Y0-EKZ-638

Mills College Library
WITHDRAWN

California Government and Politics

ANNUAL

1995 - 1996

CALIFORNIA
JOURNAL
PRESS

Copyright© 1995 by Information for Public Affairs, Inc.
    Published by California Journal Press, 2101 K Street,
    Sacramento, CA 95816.

All rights reserved. Printed in the United States of America.
    No part of this publication may be reproduced or
    transmitted in any form or by any means, electronic or
    mechanical, including photocopy, recording, or any
    information storage and retrieval system without permission
    of the publisher except by a reviewer who wishes to quote
    brief passages in connection with a review written for
    inclusion on a magazine, newspaper or broadcast.
ISBN: 0-930302-30-3
ISSN: 0084-8271

320.47
C153
1995-1996

INTRODUCTION

The California Phenomenon

The California system of government is the same in bold outline as the government of the United States, with three theoretically equal branches of government operating under the supreme law of the land, the Constitution. Nevertheless, there are some significant differences:

• The California Constitution is far more detailed than the United States Constitution and, thus, the Governor and the Legislature have far less power and freedom than the President and Congress. Matters that are left to the statute-writers in Washington are covered in detail in the California Constitution, taking these issues out of the hands of the Governor and Legislature. The judiciary, on the other hand, may be even more powerful because this branch is in charge of interpreting the constitution.

• Normally, the speaker of the Assembly has far more power in Sacramento than any single member of Congress in Washington because this official controls virtually all committee appointments. Few bills pass over the speaker's objection. However the power of particular speakers ebbs and flows depending on factors such as their personalities, the size of their party's majority and the loyalty of their parties caucus. Moreover, under Prop. 140's term limits, speakers succeeding Willie Brown will not be as powerful because they will have a much shorter term in that office.

• The people at large have much more control over California government than over national government because they have the powers of initiative, referendum and recall, giving them the ultimate voice in all matters that are not in conflict with the United States Constitution. Most major fiscal decisions, such as the enactment of general-obligation bond issues and the raising of local taxes, also cannot be made without voter approval.

Other factors make California unique as well. It has been the land of superb climate, breathtaking natural scenery, rapid growth, and the glamor of movie stars and the radio and television industries. Its government and politics reflect the excitement of a land of opportunity and colorful characters, and the news media look to California for the bizarre and offbeat. These unique characteristics may be fading, however. No longer is California the promised land; smog has dulled the horizon; unemployment runs higher than elsewhere; and the movie industry is far from what it used to be. California is experiencing the ills of a mature society: slowed financial growth, reduced national defense spending with the end of the Cold War, declining infrastructure, burgeoning population, especially among new immigrants from foreign lands, and the need for urban renewal. The Los Angeles race riot of 1992 (the worst ever in the nation), sparked by the beating of African-American Rodney King by four white police officers and their acquittal by a Simi Valley jury, is indicative of California's urban malaise. California, in short, is no longer the land of milk and honey.

Constitution

Every few years the California Legislature prints a paperback book with up-to-date versions of the United States and California Constitutions. The document that is the basic law of the entire nation takes up 27 pages; but the California Constitution takes up three times as much space (and twice as much just for the index).

The state constitution contains 21 articles describing, in great detail the bill of rights, the powers of various branches of government and basic state law in such fields as education, local government, corporations, taxation, water, harbor frontages, state debt, homesteading, motor vehicles, civil service, open space, public housing, and even the minimum drinking age.

The California Constitution wasn't always such a long-winded document. The first constitution, adopted in 1849 (one year before California was admitted into the Union),

MILLS COLLEGE
LIBRARY

was a basic statement of the rights of the people and the responsibility of the three branches of government. Peter H. Burnett was elected California's first governor in November 1849, and the first Legislature convened shortly thereafter to levy taxes, establish cities and counties, put the courts into operation, and borrow enough money to grease the wheels of state government. Over the next 30 years, only three major changes were made to this constitution. This stands in sharp contrast to the current practice of adopting amendments every election year.

Massive unrest produced a greatly expanded new constitution in 1879. There was tremendous distrust of the state government, especially the Legislature, and demands were made for greater public control over taxation. The state's population had increased 17-fold in its first three decades. A drought and unfavorable economic conditions had produced mass unemployment. The railroad bloc practically ran the state and was an obvious target. Farmers were in revolt against the railroads and other businessmen. Unemployed whites joined the Workingman's Party to seek a ban against imported Chinese labor. Constitutional reform was seen as a solution, and a convention was called in 1878. The result was an extremely detailed document, which was adopted the next year by a comfortable but not overwhelming margin. The document remains the basic law of California, although it has been amended hundreds of times.

But despite the goals of those who demanded the convention, the second constitution did not provide major reform. That was to come later with Hiram Johnson and the Progressives, who instituted the initiative, referendum and recall.

Amending the Constitution

There are three ways amendments to the California Constitution may be placed on the ballot for approval by a majority of the voters: by initiative petition now requiring nearly 700,000 signatures of registered voters, by legislative proposal, and by constitutional convention.

• *The initiative*. Almost every election California voters decide the fate of one or more measures placed on the ballot through the initiative process. The initiative was designed as a method of exerting public control over the Legislature, so that bills ignored by the lawmakers could be put into effect. In recent years, elected officials themselves have sponsored initiatives when they are unable to get their way in the Legislature. Beginning in the late 1970's the initiative has been used more and more frequently by special interest groups, the very element the initiative was created to counter. The initiative can also be used to enact statutes.

• *Legislative proposal*. Every year, legislators introduce dozens of proposed constitutional amendments. A small percentage receive the necessary two-thirds vote of each house to qualify for the ballot. A 1983 law requires that ballot measures be numbered consecutively from election to election, starting with November 1982, to avoid confusion. Thus, for example, the November 1994 ballot measures were numbered 181 to 191.

• *Convention*. The constitution provides that the Legislature may call a constitutional convention by a two-thirds vote of both houses. However, it has not done so since 1878. Instead the Legislature has chosen to form a revision commission because it can control the commission and its recommendations. Such a commission existed from 1963 to1970. The commission had some successes during those years and managed to reduce the size of the constitution considerably. A new constitutional commission was established in 1994 to evaluate and recommend structural reforms in California government. 🏛

The Abiding Dream

By Lou Cannon

Reprinted from *California Journal*, January 1995

alifornia has long been celebrated as a land of limitless possibilities, but the current wisdom is that the state's best days are history and that the shining, California dream is dead.

Three years ago *Time* magazine devoted an entire issue to a blunt obituary called "California: The Endangered Dream." Since then, the state has survived drought, riots, fires and earthquakes while suffering from business exodus, white flight, and hyperbolic fears of being overwhelmed by illegal immigrants. Public opinion surveys by venerable California pollster Mervin Field have found record levels of pessimism.

"Everywhere you go, you see people giving up on California," said Kevin Starr, one of the few historians who does not share this pessimism.

Certainly, the implicit premise of the 1994 gubernatorial race was that the good life is gone in California. Republican Governor Pete Wilson blamed immigrants, crime and a federal government that mandates programs without paying for them. Democratic challenger Kathleen Brown blamed Wilson and declining opportunities. Wilson won handily, partly because he has been a capable governor under difficult circumstances and partly because his campaign was as skillful as his opponent's was inept. But even Wilson acknowledges that California faces continuing hard times.

> "With our diverse population and the kind of new businesses that are being generated, we could become the first universal nation."
> —James K. Didion

What has happened to California's fabled optimism? Is the California dream susceptible of restoration or is it destined to be only a memory of a happier time when solutions to the state's problems seemed within the grasp of its citizens and their political system? These questions are the subject of this essay, which examines issues of population, immigration, economic change and political attitudes as they relate to the California dream.

The dream was born in 1848, when California exploded into national consciousness with the discovery of gold, the enduring international symbol of wealth and independence.

A poor man's gold rush ensued, bringing risk-takers to California from every corner of the globe. As Carey McWilliams observed, the discovery of gold coincided with a revolution in transportation and communication that made mass migration possible, "catapulted California into the national limelight ... increased its population 2500 percent in four years" and gave it statehood within two years.

The state has been on the cutting edge of change ever since. Elsewhere in America, economic and political development gradually accelerated as energy accumulated. "But in California," wrote McWilliams, "the lights went on all at once, in a blaze, and they have never been dimmed."

From California's adventurous beginnings the state became a magnet for immigrants of energy and talent from every race and ethnic group. Other "gold rushes" followed, attracting new waves of risk-takers: the "green gold" of agriculture, the "black gold" of oil, the dream machine of the movies, and the war machine of defense and aerospace.

Individualism was the social corollary of economic opportunity. Entrepreneurs were valued and honored. Politicians were nourished on the cult of "the man, not the party." William Faulkner had defined the American dream as "a sanctuary on earth for individual man," and the California dream was the American dream writ large and made accessible to everyone. "Mister, this is dreamland," declared a *Life* article in 1943 that described how Southern California was "irresistibly attractive to hordes of people."

The entire population of the state was then seven million people, and even the most visionary Californians could not foresee the full dimensions of the boom to come. When social historian McWilliams in 1949 wrote "California: the Great Exception," from which the comments attributed to him in this article are taken, he anticipated an "eventual"

population of 20 million.

The eventuality arrived by 1970 without dimming California optimism. When newly re-elected Governor Ronald Reagan delivered his State of the State message in 1970, an address reprinted in the first issue of *California Journal*, he talked almost routinely about preserving "the magic of California."

But a quarter century later, the magic seems to have disappeared, without anyone knowing quite where it went or when it vanished. Some believe that the magic is a casualty of overcrowding. California extends 800 miles from corner to corner, and its size enabled it to absorb early waves of immigration with relative ease. But the population pessimists contend that the state will soon exceed its carrying capacity, or, at a minimum, that the easy-going California lifestyle will be damaged beyond recognition.

Finding living space for new residents has been a California preoccupation since the early days of the century. The historic response of urban planners to population pressure was to spread out, providing cheap homes for newcomers at the cost of farmland and desert. Los Angeles became "40 suburbs in search of a city" and was emulated in the suburban sprawl of the Inland Empire and the Santa Clara Valley.

The suburbanizing process encouraged an automobile culture that was simultaneously egalitarian and destructive. The sprawling city-suburbs provided inexpensive and often comfortable housing for millions of working-class and middle-class Californians whose home equities became passports to prosperity. But the atomized communities in which they lived were too often unsatisfactory pseudo-cities inhabited by weary commuters who left before dawn to reach their work places and arrived home after dark on congested freeways that clogged the skies with smog.

In today's California, that commute is actually changing for the better. Business decentralization and telecommunication have brought work places nearer, reduced driving distances, and encouraged a new sense of community. Meanwhile, after succeeding in the San Francisco Bay Area, rapid transit finally has caught on in Southern California, where bus and light rail use is expanding faster than automobile traffic. *Time's* report on the endangered dream declared that "mad, fit joggers must run at night if they hope to breathe freely," but Southern California smog levels are lower than in the '70s, when the dream was flourishing, and they are likely to decline even more with the recent introduction of reformulated gasoline.

Weighing more heavily on the dream than population pressure has been the bitter dispute over population composition, much of it framed as a debate about illegal immigration. An analysis of driver's license records in 1992 showed a record exodus of 580,000 persons from California and prompted *The Sacramento Bee* to suggest renaming the state song, "California, There They Go."

The exodus has been primarily of white, middle-class and older Californians. High birth rates, particularly among young immigrants, have pushed California's population above 32 million and increased tax burdens to pay for the schools and social services.

It is not a new problem. *Newsweek* magazine, in a 1948 article called "Crowded California," said that "climate-minded, population-conscious, real-estate mad California has burst its breeches" and "is suffering from the worst case of economic growing pains in American history..."

These growing pains did not trouble three-term Republican Governor Earl Warren, who was quoted by the magazine as saying that California was getting "the greatest population bargain in history." When it was pointed out that most newcomers were young families with debts, Warren said, "I would rather have the production of the best years of the young people now migrating to our state than the dollars the retired people earned elsewhere."

Now, however, young foreign-born immigrants are becoming part of the economy without becoming part of the electorate. Latinos are 26 percent of California's population and 14 percent of registered voters but, according to *Los Angeles Times* exit polls, were only 8 percent of those who cast ballots in last November's election. This minimal participation assured passage of Proposition 187 and abetted scapegoating of illegal immigrants before and after the campaign.

Studies by the Urban Institute, RAND and Los Angeles County impeach the widely held notion that illegal immigrants cost more than they contribute. But the economic contributions (largely Social Security taxes that are collected and never repaid as benefits) are distributed nationally while costs of social services are disproportionately shouldered by border states and counties.

A historic dark side of the California dream has been the scapegoating of minorities during economic crises. When Chinese imported to work on the transcontinental railroad competed for jobs during a recession in the 1870s, labor agitators raised the cry, "The Chinese must go." Chinese were denounced at rallies and lynched by mobs. In successive decades this agitation was extended to imported Japanese, Filipino and Korean workers and to Mexicans brought in as farm workers. The latter were imported during the labor shortages of the two world wars but rounded up and dumped at the Mexican border during the Depression.

The reputations of two great California leaders — Progressive Hiram Johnson and Warren — were blemished by racial demagoguery. As governor in 1913, Johnson signed the Anti-Alien Land Act, which prohibited Japanese ownership or tenancy of agricultural land. As state attorney general in 1942, Warren participated in efforts to intern Japanese-Americans during World War II, an action retrospectively recognized as disgraceful and unjustified.

Governor Pete Wilson's popular campaign against illegal, mostly Latino, immigrants is reminiscent of these sad episodes, which also were immensely popular at the time. And like anti-Chinese agitation, the Anti-Alien Land Act and the Depression exportation of Mexicans, the present demonizing of illegal immigrants is a byproduct of economic frustration.

The collapse of the Cold War triggered aerospace layoffs, punctured the overblown California real estate boom, sent the state into its worst economic slump since the Depression and arguably did more to diminish the California dream than any other single event. Aerospace workers were the elite troops of a work force made necessary by hot and cold wars. From the military buildup before World War II until the demise of the Soviet Union a half century later, the defense industry was an economic cornucopia for California, providing so many jobs that a myth arose that the state was recession-proof. "The California economy was on steroids," said Starr.

Then the aerospace collapse rippled through the California economy, accounting for one-fourth of the 800,000 jobs lost in the state during a three-year period that began soon after Wilson took office. But the structural economic changes caused by the aerospace collapse were even more significant than the job losses.

The structural change can be illustrated by a comparison of aerospace to the apparel industry, the state's fastest-growing manufacturing sector during the economic downturn. In 1993 the median aerospace wage rate was $45,000 a year compared to $34,000 for all California manufacturing jobs. But the median wage in apparel, with a heavily Latino and Asian work force, was only $17,000 a year. While more than two and one-half garment jobs were needed to equal the purchasing power of a single lost aerospace job, aerospace declined at about the same rate that apparel manufacturing was growing.

Reporting on the California economy for *The Washington Post* in 1993, I interviewed Southern California aerospace workers while my colleague Jessica Crosby talked to Spanish-speaking garment workers in the Los Angeles apparel district. Many of the aerospace workers were disillusioned by crime, congestion and lack of economic opportunity. They talked of retiring, retraining for other work or leaving California. The garment workers,

Detail Computer illustration by Perry Babasin

while working for low wages under poor conditions, were imbued with the ambitions of immigrants: education for their children, a home or a car, a chance to make something of themselves.

"I want everything," said Hugh Gonzalez, 22, who had come to Los Angeles from Guadalarjara. He cut out vest patterns on a hand-held machine by day, attended night school to improve his rudimentary English and said he wanted to become a veterinarian.

Reading such interviews, I realized that the garment workers were as captivated by the California dream as any 19th Century gold-seekers. Soon afterward I discussed this with Assemblyman John Vasconcellos (D-San Jose), who said: "A new society is emerging in California, but its shape isn't clear. We're in a chasm between two shores. We can't go back to the shore we've left, and the other is too far away for us to see it clearly."

While 1994 was the year of Proposition 187, it was also the year when the Greater San Diego Chamber of Commerce (and the *San Diego Union*) opposed the measure in part because of its potential damage to U.S.-Mexican relations. It was the year when the North American Free Trade Agreement proved its worth and when the General Agreement on Tariffs and Trade was approved by Congress. It was a year of vast expansion of trade with nations of the Pacific Rim, California's natural partners as the tide of the commerce continues westward.

The private sector clearly must provide leadership if California is to navigate the shoals of cultural change and reach the other shore, for the public has lost confidence in the government solutions that were widely accepted a quarter century ago.

When *California Journal* for its 20th anniversary issue asked prominent Californians to look ahead at the next two decades, Reagan talked about increased telecommuting, work decentralization and "privitization of many functions of government." Jerry Brown said the Russian concept of *perestroika* would become a metaphor for worldwide restructuring.

Their comments were prescient, perhaps because both Reagan and Brown had advanced variants of these ideas during their governorships. Under Reagan, the growth of the state work force slowed for the first time since World War II. Brown advocated an "era of limits" that voters enforced in 1978 with Proposition 13, the initiative that ignited the nationwide anti-tax revolt and still restricts public expenditures in California.

Diminished government and the anti-politics revolution is a worldwide phenomenon. The seminal event was the collapse of the Soviet Union, which reduced the perceived need for a powerful, intrusive and military-oriented U.S. government and arguably had as much impact on national public attitudes as the aerospace collapse had on the California economy.

According to Department of Finance projections, California's population will surpass 40 million by 2006, reach 50 million by 2022 and 60 million by 2036. Latinos will become the largest ethnic group in the state by 2020. By 2002, the state will have no racial or ethnic majority.

"Look at it another way," said Vasconcellos. "By the year 2010, three-fourths of the people on retirement will be Anglo whites and two-thirds of the work force supporting our retirement will be people of color."

Can California deal with such changes? Versions of this question have been put to Californians ever since the gold mines gave out, and the answers have always been affirmative.

The best answers today come not from think tanks but from the sweat of people such as Alicia Aguilar, an immigrant from Toluca, Mexico, who works 11 hours a day making blouses at piece-work rates in a Los Angeles garment factory that is literally a sweatshop because of the lack of air conditioning. Aguilar's three children are learning English, however, and they will be part of the new California.

Answers also are coming at the other end of the economic spectrum by the growing high-tech health care industry, which in California today accounts for nearly 150,000 jobs. "The state has a toehold in the industries of the future," said Kirk West, president of the California Chamber of Commerce.

James K. Didion, chief executive officer of CB Commercial Real Estate Group of Los Angeles and a lifelong Californian, believes that the state's natural advantages and the "renewal of energy" provided by legal immigration will lead to a California revival.

"I look back with great nostalgia to the way California used to be," said Didion. "But with our diverse population and the kind of new businesses that are being generated, we could become the first universal nation. California's future could be even brighter than its past."

That is what Reagan believed a quarter century ago. Delivering his State of the State message in 1970, Reagan said: "We seek ways to accommodate those who want to share in the magic of California without allowing that magic to be swept away by a wave of people and pollution."

The accommodation is still being sought despite more pollution and many more people. The magic of California is being rediscovered. The dream abides. 🏛

Lou Cannon is a veteran political reporter and the author of numerous books, including "President Reagan, the Role of a Lifetime." He currently is writing a book on the aftermath of the Los Angeles riots and the Rodney King trial and is on leave from The Washington Post.

O California

by Richard Reeves

Reprinted from *California Journal*, January 1995

what plagues the Lord has visited upon us! The sun and the sea brought outsiders from the East and Europe with their money and talent and ambition — and their children who had to be educated in our schools. War brought the military and their billions upon billions of dollars — and then they said they did not need all the bombs and planes and rockets anymore. The water from other parts made the desert bloom — and we needed those damn Mexicans to pick all that green gold.

O California! Such suffering when surely the world owes us a living.

I left California after Proposition 13 but came back in time for Proposition 187. So I feel qualified to comment on the horrors that made us rich as our little properties became worth hundreds of thousands, even millions of dollars without us doing a lick of work. Those people came from the South to blow the leaves away from our lawns before the sprinklers could wet them and make them soggy, like the leaves in other places. Then those Japanese came, trying to push us around by investing billions of dollars in California companies and real estate — $7.4 billion in 1990 alone and wasn't that terrible?

Then there was Washington. The federal government just would not get off our backs, sending all those defense contracts and, usually, sending $1.25 for every $1.00 collected in taxes out here. And, usually, we complained that there should have been more. The voice of the people in the Golden State is, more often than not, wail or whine.

It was heard in the land after last year's Northridge earthquake. The epicenter legislator was Assemblywoman Paula Boland (R-Granada Hills), whose home was so damaged that she had to move into her car until the building could be shored up. Surveying the wreckage with Governor Pete Wilson, she declared that government had to do something about this. The federal government, she meant. What about the state? "No," she said. "Californians are already paying too much in taxes. ...The federal government owes us because of the all the defense cutbacks."

There it is. From the beginning of World War II until the end of the Cold War, the people of the rest of the United States — called taxpayers — poured billions into the defense and aerospace industries. They subsidized us not because of the native virtues of Californians; they did it because the weather is so good in Southern California that planes can fly in the sun almost every day of the year and because mountains of material can be stored outdoors all year, something not possible in, say, Minnesota, and because California is so vast and so much of it is desert that scientists, technicians and soldiers could make a lot of noise out there without disturbing too many people. Boom!

Boy, was California lucky! "Southern California is, in many respects, a creation of the Pentagon," says Allen J. Scott, the director of UCLA's Center for Regional Policy Studies. There was a time when 43 percent of the manufacturing jobs in Los Angeles and Orange counties were serving one customer, the United States government. In San Diego County, Wilson's home, it was 75 percent. But don't bother Ms. Boland or the governor with that kind of talk; all they want to hear and say is that since the fall of the Berlin Wall, Washington has taken 60,000 aerospace jobs away from California.

Granted, politicians do not speak for all of us. And the quality of California pols has decreased noticeably over recent years. Here is an exchange between Assembly Speaker Willie Brown Jr. and Los Angeles County Supervisor Gloria Molina, both Democrats, during last year's budget negotiations. Said he: "You scalawags ... Greedy! ... Los Angeles would squeal no matter how much you gave them." Said she: "We should look at all ways possible to stick it to Sacramento."

But the fault is not in our politicians but in ourselves. California is the people you see on television after every natural disaster. My favorites are movie producers in Malibu lamenting the loss of their weekend places, at sea now or covered with the mud of the sliding Santa Monica Mountains. It's not their fault that they built on a fault or shifting sands. Where's the money to rebuild? What's wrong with those people in Washington and Sacramento? They should be here to fix this up and, by the way, when is the National Guard going to be mobilized to find my cat, Buffy?

Having said that, I love the place. In 1966, when I first stepped off a plane at LAX and saw palm trees and heard their clack-clack sound in the wind — I'd never actually believed they were real — I had the same reaction as Henry James had in 1905: "The charming sweetness of and comfort of this spot have completely bowled me over — such a delicious difference to the rest of the United States do I find it."

And it got better. In the early 1970s, the British magazine *The Economist* sent a team of writers west to write a long survey of California life, serious people who studied the numbers and the productivity of the place and concluded it had become one of the great economies and production machines in world history. But with a difference. Parodying Lincoln Steffens' praise of the Soviet Union — "I have seen the future and it works!" — this crew began their California survey by saying, "We have seen the future and it plays!"

Those were the laid-back days. I lived here then, in Pacific Palisades, where Ronald Reagan lived. You could drive from the center of town to the beach in a minute. It was right down the hill on Temescal Canyon Road, a wide new street built through the ranch that Debbie Reynolds and Eddie Fisher owned when they were married. They put Pacific Palisades High School in there, too, overlooking the Pacific, and when kids graduated, most of them went on to the University of California, one of the best universities in the world — free.

There were old jobs and new companies, and everyone seemed to be getting richer as the land and the houses on it became more and more valuable day by day. Property value and incomes were growing so fast that the state government was getting so much money it did not know what to do with it after the new schools were built and the roads were as smooth as could be. Life was perfect in the free sunshine. Or so it appeared. And, in California, appearance is everything.

It was easy to think nothing could go wrong here. And if bad things do happen, it must the fault of outsiders or, worse, foreigners. There is something about the excess of pleasure in sweet California air that drives Californians to political excess. Burn out the Chinese now that the railroad's built. Stop the Okies at the border. Lock up the Japs and divide up their land. Round up the Mexicans and send them back where they came from.

Then a funny thing happened on the way to the 1980s. Rising real estate prices, 50 percent and more a year from 1975 to 1978, were making homeowners rich — on paper. But their property taxes were inflating at the same rate — and that was in cash. Politicians let the money pile up in the capital, Sacramento, a golden pile higher than $5 billion — while people with relatively fixed incomes worried about losing their homes because they could not pay the exploding taxes. A lot of Californians were mad as hell and they got behind an old Howard Jarvis, who invented Proposition 13. A tax revolt. It was approved by 65 percent of state voters on June 6, 1978, and became Article XIIIA of the state constitution, effectively capping the property taxes of the people who were already here and making it damned near impossible to raise other taxes.

Proposition 13 worked — and then some. The oldtimers got to keep their homes and pay a fraction of the taxes newcomers pay. In parts of the state, for identical homes on the same block, new homeowners pay 20 times the taxes paid by old timers — and some projections show that ratio reaching 70-to-1 after the year 2000.

"Stays put" is in the language of Article XIIIA. It's what old people do in what used to be the land of the young and the mobile. Older Californians are staying put and new laws make it possible for them to pass on their Proposition 13 tax breaks to their children. It's the modern equivalent of a hereditary royal grant. If that seems unfair or foolish — in the same way New York City's rent-control laws raised other housing prices and forced young families out of the city — the director of the Howard Jarvis Taxpayers Association, a fellow named Joel Fox, told me that whatever pain there is only lasts for awhile. "You feel better in a few years," he said, "because the next buyer on the block will pay even more than you did."

Nice. The Seventy-eighters, their children and often their grandchildren educated in good schools backed by the wealth of California property, voted to trade lower property taxes for themselves in exchange for diminished education spending for other people's children — many of them, it happens, black and Hispanic kids. Now we have Proposition 187, approved overwhelmingly last year (and providing that Joel Fox was probably right) to allow us to throw a lot of Hispanic kids out altogether.

So, where are we going? South, as in Mississippi. Before Proposition 13, California routinely ranked in the top five of kindergarten-through-12th grade (K-12) educational spending — and achievement — but since then has steadily dropped into the bottom 10 of the 50 states. Classroom size is now the largest in the country and per-capita spending for the state's five million public school students last year was roughly $4600, more than $1000 less than the national average and half the spending in states like New York and New Jersey. The schools passed another milestone in decline this year when U.S. Department of Education reading test scores showed California fourth-graders tied for last-in-the-nation, with Mississippi, once seen as the heart of American darkness.

California, alas, blinded by gold and sun, has chosen the old over the young. The old chose themselves. We chose ourselves over our children and someday they will hate us for it. ⌂

Richard Reeves is an author and syndicated columnist based in Los Angeles. His seven books include the bestselling Convention *and* American Journey: Traveling with Tocqueville in Search of Democracy in America. *His writing ap-pears regularly in* The New Yorker *and* The New York Times Magazine.

EXECUTIVE BRANCH & BUDGET

California's governor has, as does the President of the United States, power that is counter-balanced by power of the other branches of government and the electorate. The governor reigns supreme in very few areas. One of them is appointments, but many of these are subject to confirmation by the state Senate. California's governor has remarkably few appointments compared to other states because the civil service system has long been established for all but the top policy posts. The governor also has prime responsibility for the fiscal affairs of state, but his budget is subject to alteration by the Legislature. The governor can reduce or eliminate items in the budget passed by the Legislature. This "line-item" veto is a very powerful tool of California Governors. These vetoes, like any others, are subject to override by two-thirds vote of the Senate and Assembly, through this happens only rarely. Former Republican Presidents Ronald Reagan and George Bush supported a line-item veto federal amendment to strengthen the executive's fiscal power. Democratic President Bill Clinton is also an admirer of the line-item veto.

Governors are elected for four-year terms, with a two-term maximum (established by Proposition 140 in November 1990). Historically, only Earl Warren was elected more than twice. The order of succession is the lieutenant governor, Senate president pro tempore, Assembly speaker, secretary of state, attorney general, treasurer and controller. The governor serves as the ceremonial chief of state, as president of the University of California Board of Regents and the State University and Colleges Board of Trustees, as unofficial leader of his party, and as the head of most administrative agencies through his subordinate appointees. The governor is deeply involved in the legislative process, through presentation of the budget, the office's veto power and the traditional presentation of a package of bills constituting a legislative program (and usually outlined in the annual "state-of-the-state" message). When stymied by the legislature, Governor Pete Wilson has also authored initiatives.

Veto power

The veto is perhaps the governors most potent weapon, but it is essentially a negative power. Governors usually wield considerable influence with members of their own party (because they often control the party structure, weak as it is, and because lawmakers like to stay on the good side of a governor so they can get projects for their districts and appointments for their friends). Consequently, vetoes are rarely overridden. When Governor Ronald Reagan had a veto overridden during the 1973-74 session, it was the first over-ride since 1946. Jerry Brown was overridden during his first term on a death-penalty measure and overrides became almost commonplace in 1979, especially on fiscal issues. Neither George Deukmejian nor Pete Wilson has had a veto overridden.

Governors have the power to organize the administrative agencies of state government as they see fit, although the Legislature can veto major reorganization plans. Reagan organized his administration into four agencies headed by the secretaries of health and welfare, business and transportation, agriculture and services, and resources. The Department of Finance reported directly to the Governor. The cabinet met regularly and established policy for the administration.

The Jerry Brown administration employed the case-study method for solving problems and establishing policies. Cabinet sessions at the start were frequent, lengthy and argumentative — far less business-like than in the Reagan years. However Brown put agency executives on a loose leash once they learned what he expected from them. Jerry Brown created a fifth agency, the Youth and Adult Correctional Agency.

George Deukmejian, it was assumed, would be willing to bargain and compromise with the legislature on issues since, as a former legislator, he was used to a give and take process. His unyielding stance during his first year in office on issues like taxes and community college fees surprised many. Despite the fact that he was the sole Republican among the state's statewide officeholders and both houses of the Legislature were Democratic-controlled, Deukmejian wielded the powers of his office with considerable effect.

Deukmejian's Republican successor, Governor Pete Wilson, selected a more moderate and pragmatic group of Cabinet secretaries. Wilson has also established three new cabinet-level agencies: Environmental Protection, Child Development and Education, and Trade and Commerce.

Sharing executive power with the governor are a number of boards and commissions. The governor appoints most of their members and they in turn exercise independent authority. Among them:

University of California of Regents. Aside from the power of the purse, the Regents control the university system.

State University Trustees. This board has less power and prestige than the UC Regents but has been seeking increased independence.

Public Utilities Commission. The PUC sets rates for public utilities and also exercises allied responsibilities.

Franchise Tax Board. This board administers the state income tax and handles other revenue matters.

State Lands Commission. This commission exercises control over the state's oil-rich tidelands and other public properties.

Fair Political Practices Commission. This powerful agency was created by voters in June 1974 to police the state's Political Reform Act covering lobbyist activities, campaign contributions and conflicts of interest.

Energy Resources, Conservation and Development Commission. This commission also went into operation in 1975. It is charged with establishing overall state power policy and with the selection of sites for new power plants.

Agricultural Labor Relations Board. This agency supervises management-labor activities for the agricultural industry.

Lottery Commission. Created by the 1984 initiative to run what is, in effect, one of the nation's largest businesses.

Citizens Compensation Commission. This governmental unit was established by voters with the adoption of Prop. 112 of June 1990. This commission is charged with setting the salary level of all state elected officials except judges.

In a special category is the *State Board of Equalization,* composed of the state controller and four members elected by district. It collects the sales tax and other levies, and supervises county administration of the property tax. From time to time, governors propose elimination of the Board of Equalization and the Franchise Tax Board in favor of creating a Department of Revenue under the governor's control.

Statewide offices

In addition to the governor, the state Constitution requires the election of seven other statewide officials. All are limited to two four-year terms by Proposition 140. See box for a list of current incumbents, the individuals they defeated and their predecessors.

Here is a brief rundown of the duties of these other statewide officials:

• **Lieutenant Governor:** presides over the Senate, serves as a member of numerous state boards and commissions, and exercises the powers of chief executive when the governor leaves the state or is incapacitated.

• **Secretary of State:** the state's chief election officer; maintains all the state's official files and historical documents, including articles of incorporation; receives lobbyists' registrations and their monthly reports; receives campaign-contribution and conflict-of-interest disclosure forms.

• **Attorney General:** the state's chief law enforcement officer, legal advisor to state agencies.

• **Treasurer:** provides all banking services for the state, including sale of bonds and investment of securities.

• **Controller:** the principal accounting and disbursement officer for the state; administers inheritance and gift taxes and performs a variety of functions assigned by the Legislature, including publication of statistics on local government.

• **Superintendent of Public Instruction:** heads the state Department of Education, but most of the public schools are administered by local boards; state education policy is established by the state Board of Education, composed of gubernatorial appointees.

• **Insurance Commissioner:** This is a relatively new position created by the passage of Proposition 103 in 1988. The commissioner oversees the operations of the state Department of Insurance and has wide authority to approve or disapprove many types of insurance rates.

Constitutional Officers

	Incumbent (year first elected)	Defeated Nov. 1994	Predecessor
Governor	Pete Wilson (R) 1990	Kathleen Brown (D)	George Deukmejian (R)
Lieutenant Governor	Gray Davis (D) 1994	Cathie Wright (R)	Leo McCarthy (D)
Secretary of State	Bill Jones (R) 1994	Tony Miller (D)	March Fong Eu (D)
Attorney General	Dan Lungren (R) 1990	Tom Umberg (D)	John Van de Kamp (D)
Treasurer	Matt Fong (R) 1994	Phil Angelides (D)	Kathleen Brown (D)
Insurance Commissioner	Chuck Quackenbush (R) 1994	Art Torres (D)	John Garamendi (D)
Controller	Kathleen Connell (D) 1994	Tom McClintock (R)	Gray Davis (D)
Superintendent of Public Instruction	Delaine Eastin (nonpartisan)1994	Maureen DiMarco	Dave Dawson*

Note: Minor-party candidates omitted.   *Acting upon conviction of a felony of Louis (Bill) Honig

GOVERNOR

ELECTED CONSTITUTIONAL OFFICERS

Lieutenant Governor
Secretary of State
Controller
Treasurer
Board of Equalization (4)
Attorney General (Department of Justice)
Superintendent of Public Instruction (Department of Education)
Insurance Commissioner

EDUCATION POLICY BOARDS

Board of Education
U.C. Board of Regents
State College and University Trustees
Community College Board of Governors
Postsecondary Education Commission
Commission for Teacher Preparation and Licensing

BUSINESS, TRANSPORTATION AND HOUSING AGENCY

Dept. of Alcoholic Beverage Control
Dept. of State Banking
Dept of Corporations
Highway Patrol
Dept. of Housing and Community Development
Dept. of Motor Vehicles
Dept. of Real Estate
Dept. of Savings and Loan
Dept. of Transportation
California Housing Finance Agency
Stephen P. Teale Data Center
Office of Traffic Safety

RESOURCES AGENCY

Dept. of Conservation
Dept. of Fish and Game
Dept. of Forestry & Fire Protection
Dept. of Boating and Waterways
Dept. of Parks and Recreation
Reclamation Board
S.F. Bay Conservation and Development Commission
Dept. of Water Resources
California Conservation Corps
Colorado River Board
Coastal Commission

HEALTH AND WELFARE AGENCY

Dept. of Alcohol and Drug Programs
Employment Development Dept.
Dept. of Developmental Services
Dept. of Health Services
Dept. of Mental Health
Dept. of Rehabilitation
Dept. of Social Services
Dept. of Aging
Office of Statewide Health Planning & Development
Emergency Medical Services Authority
Health & Welfare Data Center
Dept. of Economic Opportunity

STATE AND CONSUMER SERVICES AGENCY

Fire Marshall
Franchise Tax Board
Dept. of General Services
Personnel Board
Dept. of Consumer Affairs
Public Employees Retirement System
Teachers' Retirement System
Dept. of Veterans Affairs
Dept. of Fair Employment and Housing
Building Standards Commission
Museum of Science and Industry

TRADE AND COMMERCE AGENCY

World Trade Commission
California Film Commission
Office of Tourism
Office of Small Business Development

YOUTH AND ADULT CORRECTIONAL AGENCY

Board of Prison Terms
Dept. of Corrections
Board of Corrections
Prison Industries Authority
Youthful Offender Parole Board
Dept. of Youth Authority

ENVIRONMENTAL PROTECTION AGENCY

Air Resources Board
Integrated Waste Management Board
Water Resources Control Board
Dept. of Toxic Substance Control
Dept. of Pesticide Regulation
Office of Environmental Health Hazard Assessment

SECRETARY OF FOOD AND AGRICULTURE

DEPARTMENT OF FINANCE

DEPARTMENT OF INDUSTRIAL RELATIONS

SECRETARY OF CHILD DEVELOPMENT AND EDUCATION

Office of Administrative Law
Office of Planning and Research
Office of Emergency Services
Office of Personnel Administration
Military Department
Office of Criminal Justice Planning
State Public Defender

INDEPENDENT COMMISSIONS

Agricultural Labor Relations Board
Arts Council
Lottery Commission
State Lands Commission
Coastal Commission
Fair Political Practices Commission
"Little Hoover" Commission
Public Employment Relations Board
Transportation Commission

CALIFORNIA EXECUTIVE BRANCH ORGANIZATION

State Finance

The governor is required by the state Constitution to present a budget each January — an estimate of the state's expenditures and revenues for the fiscal year starting the following July 1st. In a state growing as fast as California, the budget increases dramatically no matter who is governor.

During the eight years Ronald Reagan was governor, the total budget doubled from $5 billion to $10 billion. Jerry Brown's first budget (1975-76) totaled $11.4 billion, and his final budget (1982-83) totaled $25.3 billion. George Deukmejian's first budget (1983-84) totaled $26.8 billion and his last budget (1990-91) was $51.4 billion. Governor Pete Wilson's 1994-95 budget totaled $55.3 billion.

These figures can be misleading because they do not show how much the cost of state government has risen. Many of the increases were for the exclusive purpose of relieving-pressure on the property tax or on local government, especially after the passage of Proposition 13 in 1978. In fact, about two-thirds of each year's budget consists of allocations to schools and other elements of local government, and about half the state budget is for public education.

Budget process

The budget process in the Legislature involves detailed study of items that are questioned by the Legislature's fiscal specialist, the legislative analyst. For months, subcommittees of the Senate Budget and Fiscal Review Committee and the Assembly Budget Committee pore over the budget and decide which items should be increased, reduced, added or eliminated. Eventually, the budget is packaged by the fiscal committees and sent to the floor of each house. As a practical matter, either the Senate or the Assembly bill becomes the vehicle for enactment of a budget. The first house to act sends its version of the bill to the other, which then puts its own figures into the legislation and sends it back to the house of origin. The changes are routinely rejected, and the budget is placed in the hands of a conference committee composed of members of both chambers. Even though the constitution requires that the budget be sent to the governor by June 15th, it is often much later before both houses are able to adopt a compromise because passage by a two-thirds majority is required.

Revenue

One major portion of the budget — estimated revenues — is not considered at all by the Legislature, except to verify that funds will be sufficient to meet anticipated expenditures. The difference between revenues and expenditures (with any carry over from the previous year taken into account) produces the projected surplus for the fiscal year.

About 75 percent of the revenue goes into the state general fund. The remaining 25 percent is collected from specific sources and placed in special funds (notably the motor vehicle fund) to be spent for specific purposes. Estimates in the governor's proposed budget for the 1995-96 fiscal year show anticipated revenue from all funds of $56.0 billion ($42.5 billion general fund; $13.5 billion special funds). Specific fund sources and their percent of total revenue are as follows:

Personal income tax, $19.5 billion (34.8%);
Sales tax, $17.4 billion (31.1%);
Bank & corporation taxes, $4.8 billion (8.6%);
Insurance, $1.3 billion (2.2%);
Motor vehicle (inc. gas tax), $7.5 billion (13.4%);
Tobacco, $634 million (1.1%);
Liquor, $270 million (0.5%);
Estate taxes, $552 million (1.0%);
Horse racing fees, $109 million (0.2%);
Other, $4.0 billion (7.1%).

Expenditures

Total proposed 1994-95 expenditures are $55.5 billion, not counting bond funds. Here are the major items of expenditure as proposed by the governor in January 1995:

Aid to schools K-12, $16.2 billion (29.2%);
Health and welfare, $15.1 billion (27.1%);
Higher education, $5.9 billion (10.6%);
Business, transportation and housing, $4.4 billion (7.9%);
Local government, $3.6 billion (6.4%);
Youth and adult corrections, $3.7 billion (6.7%);
Other, $6.6 billion (12.1%).

While the Legislature can revise the budget in any way it sees fit, the governor has only two choices when he receives the bill act at the end of June: he can veto it in its entirety and thus force the Legislature to pass a new bill, or he can reduce and eliminate specific items (this is known as blue-penciling the budget through line-item veto). This latter is the practice traditionally used.

Until the budget is enacted, the Legislature cannot pass appropriations measures unless the governor provides a letter saying that the expenditure is needed on an emergency basis. Once the budget is passed, however, the Legislature can — and usually does — send the governor numerous bills containing appropriations. The governor can cut the entire appropriation or reduce the amount. (Each of these bills can contain only a single appropriation.) 🏛

Run, Pete, Run

Governor officially "exploring" presidential run

by Steve Scott

Reprinted from *California Journal*, May 1995

Throughout his 29 years in elective office, Pete Wilson has presented many faces to the electorate: pragmatic concilliator and flinty obstructionist; environmental hawk and business apologist; advocate of an active public sector and crusader against "big government." In short, he's been a tough guy to pin down philosophically. There is one guiding principle, however, that California's ambitious governor has followed throughout his career; in fact, it borders on a mantra.

Never park in one spot too long, and always leave some time on the meter.

In 1971 Wilson left a year on his third Assembly term when he won election as mayor of San Diego. Three years into his third term as mayor, Wilson left for the U.S. Senate. He was only a few months into his second Senate term when he announced for governor, and left four years on that second term when he won the 1990 gubernatorial race. And now, with Republican majorities in both houses of Congress, and a sweet re-election victory behind him, Pete Wilson is once again giving orders for a course change. Breaking last year's oft-repeated promise to serve out his second term as governor, Wilson told a group of supporters late last month that he plans to run for president.

"Some things are right, some are plainly wrong," Wilson told the gathering, offering up the central theme which will be repeated *ad nauseum* for the next year and a half.

Wilson didn't formally announce his candidacy — so far, all he's done is to set up the obligatory "exploratory committee." In truth, however, Wilson is in the race. Staff is being brought on board, fund raisers are being scheduled, and a strategy is being plotted. Wilson himself conceded that he did not form the committee "to explore reasons not to run," and, in fact, a formal announcement is expected sometime this month. He will join a field that includes U.S. Senators Robert Dole of Kansas, Phil Gramm of Texas, Arlen Specter of Pennsylvania and Richard Lugar of Indiana, as well as former Tennessee Governor Lamar Alexander, Congressman Bob Dornan of California, television commentator Patrick Buchanan, and radio talk-show host Alan Keyes.

In making the decision, Wilson and his advisors exude a confidence bordering on bravado, and who can blame them? To win the presidency in 1996, all Wilson has to do is jumpstart a national campaign organization, raise a $20 million stake, qualify for matching funds, overcome the head starts enjoyed by virtually all his prospective GOP foes, win primaries in states where nobody ever heard of him, control a national convention, learn to debate, and beat an incumbent president who, while damaged politically, is as skillful a campaigner as ever kissed a baby. Oh yes, he also has to run a budget-challenged, racially-querulous, disaster-magnet of a state at the same time.

"Done the wrong way," understates veteran Democratic campaign consultant Darry Sragow, "the Wilson campaign could be a terrible disaster."

Just how big a disaster it could be was hinted at in Wilson's first East Coast swing as a semi-official presidential wanna-be. Like an arrogant rookie frozen by his first look at a big league curve, Wilson struggled to answer a barrage of questions about his past: tax increases, abortion, his support for Gerald Ford over Ronald Reagan in 1976, and especially, his broken promise not to run for president. His post-announcement appearance on ABC's "This Week with David Brinkley" was a halting embarassment, and he was even pinned down on "the promise" by the genial Charlie Gibson of ABC's "Good Morning America." While Wilson was wriggling back East, conservative Republicans gathered in his hometown of San Diego were using words like "betrayal" to describe his campaign.

Most other politicians might be having second thoughts after such a shaky start, but for Wilson it's practically a good omen. No politician in the race, with the exception of Bill Clinton, has been more consistently underestimated than Pete Wilson. In truth, there are several practical reasons why a Wilson campaign makes sense — for Wilson, for California, and for the Republican Party.

• *The timing's right.* Wilson has never ridden higher than now: He won re-election going away and his approval rating is up. He also boasts a resume that includes experience at all levels of government. In short, he's the insider's "outsider." "He works hard, he's got some vision, and he's got a track record," says GOP political consultant Eileen Padberg. At 61, Wilson's opportunities are dwindling, and an opportunity like this won't knock again.

• *Good issues on which to run.* As he did with immigration in 1994, Wilson has surged ahead of the curve on affirmative action this year (see *CJ*, March 1995). He has made oppressive federal mandates into an intergovernmental Boston Tea Party. As Californians have become aware, nobody milks an issue like Pete Wilson.

• *The opposition.* Wilson himself cites the quality of the opposition as a primary reason for running. With the Dan Quayles, Jack Kemps, and Bill Bennetts out of the race, Wilson's backers say he benefits by comparison with other Republicans in the race. "There is a sense with the current crop that there's a candidate missing," says veteran GOP consultant Sal Russo. Wilson is also considered a favorite among his fellow GOP governors; he's already gotten help from governors Bill Weld of Massachusetts and Christine Whitman of New Jersey.

• *He's got a good campaign team.* Veteran Wilson hands, among them spokesman Dan Schnur, campaign

Wilson Inauguration, 1994

consultant George Gorton and pollster Dick Dresner, are already hard at work on the presidential race, and national GOP fund raiser Margaret Alexander has been added to help dial for dollars. The team is smart, effective and knows its candidate well.

• *He's an effective, disciplined candidate.* Wilson's raised millions of dollars with and without campaign contribution limits, and is considered a cinch to raise the money needed to run. He is also very smart, with a knack for "seeing around the corner" to spot issues that will resonate in an election, along with a bulldog tenacity. "He has an iron butt," says GOP strategist Steve Merksamer. "The 'iron butt' generally wins the race." He is also about the best there is at sticking to his central themes — what the political pros call "staying on message."

• *He could match up well against President Clinton.* It's hard to find anyone — Democrat or Republican — who believes Bill Clinton can win re-election without winning California's 54 electoral votes. Although Wilson is anything but wildly popular in his home state, a pro-choice Californian on the GOP ticket makes Clinton's objective of winning California a whole lot tougher.

For every compelling reason why a Wilson candidacy makes sense, there is at least one compelling reason why such a candidacy could wind up, in Sragow's words, "a disaster."

• *"The Promise."* Time and again in 1994, Wilson repeatedly said he would not run for president, a pledge he now concedes he "regrets." While breaking a similar promise didn't hurt Bill Clinton in 1992, Arkansas isn't California.

Wilson with Dan Lungren, Bill Jones and Charles Quackenbush (left to right)

Wilson gives up some important moral high ground if the very act of announcing for the presidency means breaking a promise to about eight million California voters.

• *His record.* In his time, Wilson has raised taxes, engaged in deficit spending, waffled on gay rights, and changed positions on the environment and affirmative action. He is an outspoken proponent of abortion rights in a party with an anti-abortion plank in its platform, and he committed the sacriledge of backing Ford over Reagan in the 1976 campaign — even if Ford *was* the incumbent president. Although he has striven mightily to re-cast himself as a conservative hardliner, Republican elephants never forget, and Democrats have already given him a nickname: "Flip Wilson."

• *He lacks a natural base in his own party.* In the 1994 gubernatorial primary, a conservative unknown named Ron Unz walked away with about a third of the vote, and when Phil Gramm crashed the state GOP convention last month, the party faithful were only too happy to help him rain on Wilson's victory parade. Republican poobahs like Attorney General Dan Lungren and former Congressman Michael Huffington worry about leaving the state in the hands of the Democratic lieutenant governor, Gray Davis (see page 10). His most loyal supporters have been in the business community, but even they are divided on this latest venture.

• *He lacks charisma.* The governor is thin-skinned, leaden on the stump and wonkish one-on-one. He was embarrassed in both of the 1994 "debates" in which he participated. His voice has a tendency to crack like that of an adolescent, which can give the impression of nervousness. These deficiencies will be magnified in the early "retail" states such as New Hampshire and Iowa, where Dole, Gramm and Buchanan have already worn down several pairs of shoes. Wilson insiders believe they can win with the same media-intensive strategy they have used in California, but New Hampshire residents have come to view personal contact with candidates as a birthright.

• *Trouble on the home front.* Both Assembly Speaker Willie Brown Jr. (D-San Francisco) and Senate President pro Tempore Bill Lockyer (D-Hayward) are already screwing in the timing devices on budget explosives being laid out for the governor. Those who remember 1992's 64-day budget stalemate will also remember that it was Wilson who was the biggest loser in the state that year. Beyond the budget, there are Wilson's tax-cut, tort-reform, and welfare-reform propos-

als, all of which will require extensive personal lobbying. His credibility as a can-do candidate could be determined, in part, by how well he fulfills those promises with a Democratic Senate and an Assembly with leadership still in flux. "We have a legislative agenda that he's set forth that we'll be hard pressed to pass if he's not here," laments Senate GOP Leader Ken Maddy (R-Fresno).

• *He could be vulnerable in California.* Essential to any Wilson strategy is winning California's winner-take-all primary, to be held six weeks after New Hampshire. Since the state's GOP primary voters tend to give their votes to the prospective winners, early success is critical. "He's going to have to win, or do very well, in New Hampshire or New York," says Russo. Even if Wilson is still in the hunt by the March 26th primary, his fate depends on who else is in the race. If Gramm is the lone conservative in a race involving Wilson and Dole, 35 percent to 40 percent of the vote could win it. With Wilson's approval ratings as governor still lower than those of President Clinton in California, there's no guarantee he'd wind up on top.

All this prognosticating, of course, comes some 10 months before the New Hampshire primary — an eternity, politically speaking. For the moment, Wilson's challenges center around manpower and money. To "max out" on federal matching funds in the primary, Wilson must raise $20 million, in $1000 chunks, and he must demonstrate fund-raising strength in at least 20 states. Sragow says candidates routinely underestimate the difficulty of this feat. "They start out thinking they'll get it out of the way early. Three months later, they're tearing their hair out." Wilson must also have a presence "on the ground" in the key primary states, an immense challenge for someone who has never run a national campaign. Wilson insiders insist their message will help them circumvent more traditional party structures. "[Issues] help you build an organization," says Schnur.

If money and manpower prove to be no problem, Wilson then gets to the question of how he matches up against his opponents. Wilson has shown he can whip up on relatively weak primary competition in California, as he did in his 1982 Senate race. The last time Wilson ran in a primary against truly competitive opposition was in the 1978 governor's race. He got killed. This year, two of his competitors — Dole and Buchanan — have already tasted the blood of a heated presidential primary, and nearly all were trudging through New Hampshire while Wilson was still dithering. So far, national polls place him in the second tier of candidates, and every public poll to date shows Wilson even trailing Dole in California. Wilson is undeterred. "I change polls," he says, confidently.

Bravado aside, it all seems an incredibly daunting proposition for a man who just finished an 18-month, $30 million re-election marathon. If there's one thing Pete Wilson does well, however, it is seize opportunity. He seized upon the weakness of a faltering incumbent U.S. Senator S.I. Hayakawa in 1982. He seized upon the paucity of choices to succeed retiring Governor George Deukmejian in 1990. And now Pete Wilson hopes to seize upon a weak field and a weak incumbent to win the ultimate prize — the presidency.

"Winning the presidency is the equivalent of climbing Mt. Everest," says Sragow. "The odds that you're going to get all the way to the top and all the way down are small, but going into it, Wilson starts off in a very good position in terms of organization and process." 🏛

California's "morphing" economy

By Susan F. Rasky

Reprinted from *California Journal*, March 1995

Economics, like all great religions, is largely a matter of faith and assertion — a constant redefining of observable phenomena to explain the past, to predict the future and to make living in the unpleasant or confusing present a little more tolerable.

This is perhaps better understood elsewhere in the country. Here in California, we have never had to bother much about complicated economic explanations or redefinitions. Until recently, we had a perfectly serviceable myth that covered all contingencies. Our mythical past was an unbroken line of successes from the gold rush, to the oil boom, to the rise of Hollywood, the flourishing of the defense industry, the emergence of Silicon Valley and the spectacular rise in real estate prices. Our future was, well, just like the past, the only uncertainty being what precise form the next boom might take. And our present punctuated how special we were. In a state that can swing so easily from the politics of Jerry Brown to the politics of Ronald Reagan, why be overly concerned about the fulminations of Mother Nature?

Three-plus years of recession that began in 1990 changed all that, prompting (quite apart from general handwringing and soul searching) a flurry of economic studies by business, academic and governmental groups attempting to assess the impact of the steep downturn and offer some perspective on what lies beyond the next one or two budget cycles.

It's not that such studies didn't exist before, but rather that none of the state's policy players and certainly none of the public felt much need to pay attention to them. Now that the economists and deep thinkers have our collective attention,

> "The value of a 25 year economic forecast is its use at the retirement roast of the person who wrote it." — Fred Silva, executive secretary, California Constitutional Revision Commission

however, the question is whether their redefinitions of the past and their unsettling visions of the future lead us to any answers about how to plan for the next quarter century while simultaneously dealing with the very real problems of the here and now.

Certainly, it would be easier to set store in what the economists say about where California is going in the long term if their studies agreed on where the state has been in the recent past. That, alas, is asking too much.

What the studies do offer is a useful cataloging of the key variables that will shape California over the next decade or so and four somewhat distinct scenarios — each partly dependent on short-term policy choices — of what the state will look like in the early part of the next century.

But first, just a little history. Californians like to view the state's ups and downs in the most extreme fashion. In the case of this recession, however, our tendency toward melodrama has some justification.

What happened here in 1990 was a confluence of forces that had been building for more than a decade. Apart from the most obvious ones, such as the end of the great real estate boom and the dramatic drop in military spending, the state began to feel the negative effects of population growth, lack of investment in infrastructure, fiscal policy reforms directed by the initiative process that decreased money available for education and other public services, and regulatory policies that made California less attractive to new businesses.

Despite their disagreement on the precise depth, scope and duration of the recession, the economists and policy analysts who have weighed in on the subject do agree that California has experienced something more fundamental than a cyclical downturn. To any lay observer, that hardly seems a startling revelation. But in the policy community, it put to rest the myth that the state's economic base was sufficiently diverse to withstand major cutbacks in national defense spending.

Among economists, the steep recession and the apparent divergence of California from national trends also forced a more serious attempt to distinguish short-term, or cyclical impacts from permanent or structural changes in the state's economy. In a report prepared last summer for the California Business-Higher Education Forum, Larry Kimbell, director of the UCLA Business Forecasting Project, pointed to a rough consensus among forecasters about which were which. He parsed it this way:

• Jobs lost from defense cuts are permanent, with no reasonable prospect for recovery of those jobs in the next decade.

• Jobs lost to corporate downsizing are permanent, hitting once-secure middle-management and white-collar jobs particularly hard both in California and the country as a whole. Kimbell estimated that 400,000 of the 600,000 jobs lost in California during the recession occured in downsizing industries, which include not only defense and aerospace, but also retail trade, commercial construction, finance, transportation and telecommunications.

• California's housing and construction industries, while suffering the longest and most depressed downturn in postwar history, will eventually join in the national recovery of these sectors, and may get an additional boost by the need for earthquake rebuilding and seismic retrofitting. New and existing home prices, which soared in the 1980s, will stabilize for a few years and then begin to rise in line with general inflation.

• Foreign trade will be one of the most important sources of long-term growth for California, picking up in the Far East as the Japanese economy recovers and accelerating with Mexico because of the North American Free Trade Agreement (NAFTA). Although Kimbell's analysis was done before the recent Peso crisis, economists at the Business Forecasting Project said the current situation does not alter their long-term outlook.

Part of the reason economists have such difficulty reaching consensus forecasts, especially for the long term, is their annoying refusal to settle upon what to measure and how to measure it. In other words, a cautionary note to the lay analyst trying to compare forecasts: even the variables are infinitely variable.

It helps a little to divide recent studies on California's economy into two broad categories — those based upon historical notions of trade, comparative advantage and market forces; and, with appropriate apology to the practitioners, those based upon an extensive collection of empirical data, which then is turned into equations and cranked through econometric models.

In the former category, again with apologies for oversimplification, put the Palo Alto-based Center for the Continuing Study of the California Economy, the Berkeley Roundtable on the International Economy, the Denver-based Center for the New West, and assorted business and trade associations whose studies reflect the concerns and priorities of their members. In the latter category put the UCLA Business Forecasting Project, the state Department of Finance, the Legislative Analyst's Office, and the state's major banks.

Illustration by Rob Wilson

Obviously, the categories overlap, and some of the recent economic studies by academic and political or civic interest groups draw from both types of analyses.

That said, the big variables look something like this:

• **Geography:** Assuming the next major earthquake does not move the Pacific coastline eastward to Arizona, California's location at the edge of the continent and on the border of two major trading nations remains a positive for the state's long-term future. J. Ian Morrison, president of the Menlo Park-based Institute for the Future, takes geographic advantage a step further. He argues that climate, specifically a true Mediterranean climate in portions of the state, will continue to make California a magnet for "the smart, rich and hopeful."

• **Population:** This is a complicated variable to estimate because it depends not just on birth and death rates, but also on assumptions about domestic migration to California, which in turn are based on assumptions about job growth in the state. Some economists are more optimistic than others. In its 1994 report, the Center for the Continuing Study of the California Economy, for instance, was quite emphatic about the long-term trend: "Given the substantial projected growth in population and jobs in the nation, there is no doubt about the finding that California will grow significantly in terms of total jobs, population and households." The report estimated that the United States would add 30 million residents between 1993 and 2005, and another 100 million in the years after 2005. "The question of California reaching a population of 40, 45 or even 50 million is more a matter of when than whether," the CCSE study concluded.

• **Demography:** This obviously is intertwined with population, but there is general agreement among economists who study the state that aging of the baby-boom generation is a fundamental driving force behind many of the changes projected between now and 2020. Those changes include not just the obvious — such as reconfiguration of the workforce, increased demands for health-care services that may not get satisfied, and strains on the Social Security and other retirement systems — but also more subtle political and social effects. What happens to the gentrified urban areas that flourished in the 1980s as boomers abandon them in search of safer and more distant suburbs, and what new political pressures emerge as boomer children reach college age and find the state's public university system more costly and seriously overcrowded?

• **Diversity and immigration:** There continues to be disagreement among and between economists and politicians about which income and service-seeking population groups are leaving or coming to California, and how much of the movement is strictly a function of the recession. What is clear, regardless of the direction national immigration policies may take in the next few years, is that sometime in the next century, all groups in California — white, African American, Latino or Asian — are going to be minorities. And if nothing else, that implies a new level of social and political tension in California as traditional alliances and antagonisms among the population groups break down and reform.

Wither California in the next 25 years?

As always in economics, there is a scenario with a statistical back-up to suit almost any vision. Stephen Levy, of the Center for the Continuing Study of California, whose forecast appears on page 61, is traditionally an optimist. But many of his prognosticating colleagues are less sanguine given what they regard as a set for fairly limited, and ultimately painful, policy choices. (Why do you think they call economics "the dismal science"?)

The following scenarios are by no means fully wrought forecasts but rather a rough categorization of views from the recent studies of the state's economy.

• **Blade Runner:** This is futurist J. Ian Morrison's grimmest vision of the path California, specifically Southern California, will take. As in the movie by the same name, it assumes "an executive high-tech city where the well-off live in a fortress environment, and beneath them, literally and metaphorically, is a multiethnic polyglot gong show which is both unsafe and unpleasant," Morrison says. Morrison has a variation on this theme in which he describes "white and cranky" baby boomers sitting in nursing homes singing "I Got You, Babe" to each other and demanding that a young multiethnic population pay for them to live in comparative luxury.

• **Texification:** This is University of California, Berkeley, Public Policy Professor John Ellwood's description of how the political and fiscal policy choices California has already made — as well as those that voters seem likely to make in the near future — turn the Golden State into a sort of Texas on the Pacific. Ellwood notes that through the mid-1960s California's rapid economic growth and high per-capita income allowed it to be a high-tax, high public-service state that invested more per capita on public projects (including schools) than the national average. Today, he says, in a view widely shared by economists, California is a moderate tax, moderate public-service state. "What we're headed to is Texas," he says. "Small government, low investment, low wages and a greater gap between rich and poor."

• **Pittsburgh:** This is the coinage of economist Eugene Smolensky, Ellwood's colleague and dean of the Graduate School of Public Policy at UC Berkeley. It embodies a bit of the "Blade Runner" and "Texas" scenarios by assuming that Los Angeles becomes so congested and unlivable that large numbers of people leave to seek better jobs and better conditions elsewhere. The optimistic result, for those who remain, is Pittsburgh after the collapse of the steel industry — a less-polluted and less-congested city with a well-developed infrastructure and an economy based on banking and finance. In other words, a new equilibrium.

• **Convergence:** For proud Californians, who glory in being, well, different, this is perhaps the least appealing view of the future. It may also be the most realistic. David Hensley, who used to be at the UCLA Forecasting Center and now works for Salomon Brothers, notes that contrary to early wisdom on the differences between California's recession and the one experienced by the rest of the country, the state is actually looking more and more like the United States as a whole. In other words, California's historical uniqueness, in economic terms, is precisely that — history.

"We've been looking at the industry and economic structure of states, and what we're finding is that rather than states cleaving toward what they do best, over the past 30 years they are overwhelmingly converging to a national norm," he says. "This is true of California, too; now more than ever and certainly more than Californians ever believed, the state is a true microcosm." 🏛

Susan F. Rasky was an award-winning journalist for The New York Times *before coming West to head the California News Service, a project of the University of California, Berkeley, Graduate School of Journalism.*

THE JUSTICE SYSTEM

The judiciary may be the most powerful of the three branches of state government because the Constitution is so detailed and because the Supreme Court has the power to strike down acts of the Legislature or initiatives that conflict with the state and federal constitutions. The court also uses its power to void acts of the executive branch that violate either a statute or the Constitution.

Under a series of forceful chief justices — among them Phil Gibson, Roger Traynor and Donald Wright — the state's highest tribunal often led the way for the United States Supreme Court. The California Supreme Court built a reputation for activism and independence with decisions that struck down the death penalty (People v. Anderson, 1972), outlawed the state's system of financing public education (Serrano v. Priest, 1971) and invalidated an anti-fair housing initiative approved by the electorate (Mulkey v. Reitman, 1966).

An activist Supreme Court has often been viewed as a second Legislature — more powerful than the first. Governor Ronald Reagan sought to reduce the activism of the court through his appointments, but one of the big disappointments of his eight years as governor was that his appointee for chief justice, Donald Wright, turned out to be another activist.

In 1977, Democratic Governor Edmund G. Brown Jr. had an opportunity to recast the court and by 1981 his appointees comprised a majority on the court. He appointed the court's first woman, Chief Justice Rose Elizabeth Bird; first black, the late Wiley W. Manuel; and first Latino, Cruz Reynoso. Bird was a highly controversial figure when she was appointed and throughout her tenure on the court. While there were many criticisms of the Bird court by conservatives, the most critical was the court's failure to allow any executions during her tenure as Chief Justice. (Polls indicate that over 80 percent of California citizens favored the death penalty.)

In November 1986, in an unprecedented election, three of the Brown-appointed liberals, Justices Bird, Reynoso and Joseph Grodin lost their confirmation elections. This enabled Governor George Deukmejian to appoint three new conservatives to the high court. These three combined with two previous appointments gave the court a conservative majority which it has retained to date.

Lower and appellate courts

The Supreme Court sits at the apex of the California judicial system. There are three lower levels — the municipal courts, the superior courts, and the district courts of appeal. Members of the Supreme Court and the district courts of appeal are appointed by the governor subject to confirmation by the Commission on Judicial Appointments (consisting of the chief justice, the attorney general and one appeals-court justice). In recent years, the commission has called for public hearings on controversial appointees. Bird was approved by a 2-1 vote following a heated public debate. Incumbent judges' names appear on the ballot at the first general election following their appointment and again at the end of each 12-year term. If the incumbent receives a majority of "yes" votes for retention, he or she has another 12-year term.

- *Municipal courts.* These local courts hear misdemeanor cases, preliminary hearings on some felony charges, small-claims actions and civil cases involving relatively small amounts of money (less than $25,000 in both municipal and justice courts).
- *Superior courts.* These countywide courts hear juvenile criminal cases, felonies, appeals from justice and municipal court decisions, and civil cases that cannot be tried in the municipal courts.
- *Courts of appeal.* These are divided into six districts (based in San Francisco, Los Angeles, Sacramento, San Diego, Fresno, and San Jose). Each division within each court contains three or four justices, with three justices normally sitting on each appeal. The court has jurisdiction over appeals from superior-court actions and decisions of quasi-judicial state boards.
- *The Supreme Court.* The state's highest court handles appeals from the district courts of appeal, although some cases can be taken directly from the trial court to the Supreme Court. In death-penalty cases, for example, appeals automatically go from the superior court to the Supreme Court. The high court also reviews orders of the Public Utilities Commission and has some appointive powers.

Judges of the municipal and superior courts are elected by the people for six-year terms. The governor fills vacancies on the municipal and superior courts. On occasion, there is a wide-open race for a judgeship, but usually the post is filled by appointment and the incumbent retains the judgeship at the ensuing election. District courts of appeal and state supreme court judges are confirmed (they face no actual opponent) in a yes or no vote of the people to twelve year terms. They also must stand for confirmation in the first state election after their appointment.

A judge may be removed or otherwise disciplined by the Supreme Court — but only upon recommendation of the Commission on Judicial Performance. Judges are also subject to impeachment and recall, but the more common disciplinary procedure is through an investigation by the commission and action by the high court.

The state Judicial Council is a 21-member board charged with the overall administration of the court system. It is headed by the chief justice, who in turn appoints most of the members. The Administrative Office of the California Courts is the staff agency charged with carrying out the council's policies and conducting research for the council.

California uses the standard jury system. Grand juries (19 citizens in most counties, 23 in Los Angeles) investigate public agencies and have the power to hand down criminal indictments. However, the state Supreme Court ruled in 1978 that preliminary (probable-cause) hearings must be held, whether or not a suspect is indicted. Trial juries usually consist of 12 registered voters, but both sides in a case can agree to a smaller panel or waive a jury and submit the case to a judge. A unanimous vote is needed for acquittal or conviction in a criminal case. 🏛

MILLS COLLEGE
LIBRARY

CALIFORNIA'S COURT SYSTEM

U.S. SUPREME COURT

CALIFORNIA SUPREME COURT

Original jurisdiction; habeas corpus, mandamus, certiorari, prohibition

DISTRICT COURTS OF APPEAL

First District	Second District	Third District	Fourth District	Fifth District	Sixth District
San Francisco	Los Angeles	Sacramento	San Bernardino San Diego	Fresno	San Jose

Original jurisdiction; writs of mandamus, prohibition, habeas corpus, ceritorari

SUPERIOR COURTS
ONE IN EACH COUNTY

Original jurisdiction; Civil-amount in controversy exceeds $15,000, mandamus, habeas corpus, equitqable relief, probate, family law and juvenile court matters. Criminal-felonies.

MUNICIPAL COURTS

ONE IN EACH DISTRICT OF MORE THAN 40,000

Civil jurisdiction; amount in controversy, $15,000 or less. Criminal: lesser misdemeanors, preliminary hearings for felonies, infractions

MUNICIPAL COURTS

ONE IN EACH DISTRICT OF 40,000 OR LESS

Civil jurisdiction; amount in controversy, $15,000 or less. Criminal: misdemeanors, preliminary hearings for felonies, infractions

JUDICIAL COUNCIL

Makes rules on judicial procedure; surveys and expedites judicial business.

COMPOSITION:
Chief Justice
Fourteen judge appointees of chief justice
Four elected by State Bar
One Assembly
One Senate

COMMISSION ON JUDICIAL NOMINEE EVALUATION

Evaluates the Governor's prospective judge candidates.

COMPOSITION:
Nineteen elected by State Bar
Six appointed by governor

COMMISSION ON JUDICIAL PERFORMANCE

Confirms or rejects appointees of Governor to Supreme Court and Courts of Appeal

COMPOSITION:
Chief Justice
Attorney General
Senior Justice on Court of Appeals

COMMISSION ON JUDICIAL PERFORMANCE

Recommends to Supreme Court censure, removal or retirement of judges

COMPOSITION:
Three judges appointed by the Supreme Court
Two lawyers elected by State Bar
Six public members—two each appointed by the governor, Assembly speaker and Senate president pro tem.

RECOMMENDATIONS, ADVICE CONFIRMATION

LINES OF APPEAL OR REVIEW

THE LUCAS COURT

Since Rose Bird's departure, the California Supreme Court has been less controversial, and less diverse

By Bob Egelko

Bob Egelko covers the state Supreme Court for the Associated Press.

Reprinted from *California Journal*, June 1994

People who have lost track of the state Supreme Court might not remember why California has no campaign funding limits for public financing of legislative elections this year. It isn't because of legislative or public opposition; in fact, 53 percent of the public voted for those changes in a 1988 initiative.

No, the reason is that the court extinguished that initiative in a 4-3 ruling last December, saying voters would have preferred the remnants of a rival measure that already had been gutted by federal courts.

Another question. "Why aren't Proposition 103 rate rollbacks moving ahead, six years after that initiative passed and three years after Insurance Commissioner John Garamendi adopted regulations and ordered hearings?"

Responsibility might be assigned to the state bureaucracy, the insurance industry or flaws in Proposition 103 itself. But the most immediate reason is that the court agreed a year ago to review the legality of the regulations, but hasn't scheduled a hearing yet or allowed Garamendi to implement rollbacks in the meantime.

Finally, why aren't new jails and courthouses being built in San Diego County with the money from a sales tax increase that was approved by a majority of the voters, under a financing system that the court seemed to have endorsed in 1982?

The reason is that a new court majority took another look in 1991 at the two-thirds vote required by Proposition 13 in 1978 for "special taxes," interpreted the requirement more broadly and struck down the San Diego measure.

Good or bad, these decisions, and the court that issued them, deserve more attention than they're getting.

Largely by upholding death sentences, the court headed by Chief Justice Malcolm Lucas for the last several years has managed to avoid the prominence and controversy that surrounded the Rose Bird court in the years leading up to the 1986 elections, when Bird and two colleagues were voted out of office. A return to a lower profile was probably healthy for the court and certainly welcomed by the justices. But the Lucas court is an important force in the state, and it's hard to understand its near-invisibility.

For example, although Justice Edward Panelli retired January 31, more than four months after announcing his plans, Governor Pete Wilson left the vacancy unfilled for months, with no criticism from his rivals. Meanwhile, the seventh seat at monthly oral arguments was occupied by a succession of appellate justices, including some Democrats.

In a year of obsession with crime and punishment, the court wasn't even mentioned during the primary elections for governor. The only candidates who seemed interested were two Democratic hopefuls for insurance commissioner, state Senator Art Torres and Assemblyman Burt Margolin; they joined some consumer groups this March in an unsuccessful request to the Deukmejian-appointed majority on the court to withdraw from an insurance case in which the former governor represented an insurance company.

The last time many legislators seem to have taken notice of the court was in 1991, when Lucas, in a ruling upholding a term-limits initiative, belittled the effect of a 38 percent cut in the Legislature's operating budget. Legislative committees rushed to propose a 38 percent reduction in the court's budget before cooler heads prevailed.

The court's funding could suffer if the governorship were won by a Democrat, who presumably would feel less affinity for the 6-1 majority of Republican appointees. But there isn't much a new governor could do about the current majority, which, barring personal tragedies or a major scandal, should be with us into the next century.

The three 1987 Deukmejian appointees who swung the court to the right — Justices John Arguelles, Marcus Kaufman and David Eagleson — all retired in less than four years, after becoming eligible for maximum retirement benefits. Their successors — Joyce Kennard, Armand Arabian and Marvin Baxter — are younger and have many years to go on the pension ladder, as does Wilson's first appointee, Ronald George, who succeeded the retiring Justice Allen Broussard in 1991.

Justice Stanley Mosk, at 81 a 30-year veteran and the only Democrat on the court, floated enough retirement rumors before the 1986 election to keep his potential opposition off balance, avoided the purge of his fellow liberals and has shown few signs of slowing down. He is the leading dissenter on the court, slightly ahead of Kennard, who established herself as the least predictable justice soon after her appointment in 1989.

As for Lucas, the 67-year-old chief justice remains the leader of the court's controlling bloc, though he no longer writes the most opinions, as he did for several years after his elevation by ex-law partner Deukmejian in 1987. He has a few years left before maximum pension eligibility, shows no obvious ill effects from a 1987 colon cancer operation, and hasn't dropped a hint about leaving.

Lucas also seems to have withstood the embarrassment of a *San Francisco Chronicle* account last November of his frequent out-of-state travels. The article disclosed that a Lloyds of London subsidiary, which had cases before Lucas' court, paid for two of his trips to overseas conferences, raising concerns about judicial ethics. Saying the trips were part of his job, Lucas asked for an investigation by the Commission on Judicial Performance, whose nine members include five judges appointed by the Supreme Court. The commission cleared him two months later, saying the unique nature of the chief justice's job should have dispelled any suggestion of illicit influence or appearance of impropriety.

Probably the harshest public evaluation of the court was another *Chronicle* article in November, concluding that the court had sunk into mediocrity since its trailblazing years of the 1950s to mid-'70s, based on interviews with scholars and assorted legal observers. Assessments like those are beyond the scope of the present article or the capability of its author, who wishes to observe only that objective standards are elusive, and it's probably more useful to examine the justices and their work in their own time.

The current court can be divided roughly into two phases. In the first three or four years, the court defined itself largely by deciding how far to go in discarding or narrowing the doctrines of the Bird court and its predecessors. Conservatives were firmly in control, but the presence of Mosk, Broussard, and later Kennard kept debate brisk and dissents relatively frequent.

Some of the biggest plums fell quickly. In 1987 the court, under the surprising authorship of Mosk, ruled that a death sentence could be imposed without proof of intent to kill, overturning the key decision in the Bird court's death-penalty reversals. The next year, majorities led by Lucas barred suits by third parties against insurance companies for mishandling or delaying claims — overruling a 1979 decision detested by insurers — and severely limited damages for wrongful firings.

As expected, the court also started giving generous readings to initiatives that the Bird court had interpreted more narrowly. The 1991 ruling in the San Diego County case, strengthening Proposition 13's clout against local taxes, was the culmination of a trend of several years. Prosecutors won longer sentences and broader rules on confessions under a 1982 crime initiative known as the Victims' Bill of Rights. The court's sympathetic view of initiatives may have saved consumer-sponsored Proposition 103 in 1989 when the justices decided to rewrite rather than discard its rollback of insurance rates.

In civil rights, where previous courts had expanded the reach of anti-discrimination laws, the Lucas court displayed its empathy for businesses and its distrust of regulatory agencies in a series of rulings by Panelli, starting in 1987, that trimmed the powers of the state Fair Employment and Housing Commission. In 1990 the court barred suits against businesses for dis-

criminating against the poor but said it would allow other claims of arbitrary bias recognized by the Bird court. Lower courts have had trouble deciphering that ruling, and it's likely to be refined in a future case.

The first phase contained a few surprises — the rejection of a "sub-minimum" wage for workers receiving tips, the upholding of a one-house legislative veto of Deukmejian's nomination of Dan Lungren as state treasurer — and one outright stunner: Over the repeated dissents of Lucas and Panelli, the remaining appointees of anti-abortion Governor Deukmejian joined their colleagues in refusing to reconsider a Bird court ruling continuing state funding for Medi-Cal abortions.

Attempts to curtail the funding were later dropped by Wilson, but the abortion issue may soon be back before the court in the form of a never-enforced state law requiring parental consent or a judge's approval for an unmarried minor's abortion. The court finally addressed the underlying privacy issue this January in a ruling upholding drug testing of college athletes; Lucas' majority opinion, a masterpiece of ambiguity, contained much talk of core values and balancing tests, but few clues about the court's approach to abortion or other privacy disputes.

The court entered its second phase around 1991, when the majority was solidified by the appointment of George, a bright and ambitious former state death-penalty lawyer, to succeed Broussard — Jerry Brown's last remaining appointee. Its task of culling the casebooks for undesirable precedents largely complete, the court enjoyed a friendly legal landscape and political security, and could set its own agenda.

At times, this included bursts of activism usually associated with more liberal courts. After a legislative attempt to declare surrogate-motherhood contracts legal and regulate them was vetoed by Wilson, the court declared one type of surrogacy legal without regulation last year. Dismissing suggestions that a contract to bear another's child for pay exploited poor women, Panelli's opinion coolly observed that poverty often induces women to take bad jobs. Kennard, dissenting from the all-male majority, said the court was devaluing the role of the birth mother.

More often, the court has stayed true to its creed of judicial restraint, deferring to the decisions of legislators, voters and trial judges. But the court has encountered some unforeseen problems in the last few years, often as the consequences of its own earlier decisions.

First and foremost was the death penalty, the downfall of the Bird court and the top priority of the Lucas court. The repeal of the intent-to-kill requirement cleared the way for a dramatic turnaround of the affirmance rate —

from 6 percent under Bird to more than 90 percent in the last four years, the highest in the nation. Critical of the previous court's second-guessing of trial judges, the new majority relied on the doctrine of "harmless error," regularly concluding that mistaken rulings could not have influenced the jury's death verdict. The concept was sometimes carried to great lengths, excusing a judge's improper refusal to let a murderer tell jurors why he deserved to live, and another judge's erroneous decision to allow evidence of a gruesome wine-bottle rape.

The court also tore into the case backlog, deciding 56 capital appeals in a single year, 12 fewer than the Bird court had resolved in seven

years. To promote efficiency and discourage repeated appeals, the court adopted time limits and other procedural restrictions, in a 1992 ruling modeled on a U.S. Supreme Court decision.

But the backlog refused to disappear, and instead changed shape: The number of Death Row inmates without lawyers rose above 100, and the average waiting period for a lawyer reached three years, as a combination of limited pay and bleak prospects discouraged experienced attorneys from accepting capital appeals. That meant cases were taking longer to reach the court, and potential new grounds for future appeals were being created. Meanwhile, the court's efforts to dismiss new claims on procedural grounds without a hearing were meeting a chilly reception when the cases arrived before federal judges, increasing the likelihood that death sentences would be reversed and cases returned to state courts for new trials.

The length and arduousness of capital cases also took time away from civil cases, held down the court's statistical output and may have spurred some justices toward retirement. A commission appointed by Lucas in 1987 had recommended shifting some of the death-penalty workload to state appeals courts, but Lucas never endorsed the idea and it's scarcely been mentioned since.

Another area that has proven more complicated than it first appeared is torts, the broad field of liability for physical, mental and financial injuries. Decisions of the early years seemed to yield some simple rules. Tort suits were not to be the primary instrument of public protection or social policy; thus, foot-dragging by insurers was to be deterred by regulators, not by private lawsuits, and crime was to be controlled by police and lawmakers, not by victims' damage suits against landowners for faulty security. Another maxim was that firm lines had to be drawn around liability, at the price of occasional harshness to individuals. So a mother who heard neighbors scream, and ran outside to see her child lying in

the street, couldn't sue a hit-and-run driver for emotional distress because she didn't see the accident. And someone who saw a lover die in a car crash caused by a drunken driver couldn't sue unless the couple was married.

This approach has the advantage of clarity and doesn't have to sacrifice an understanding of human problems. One of the court's most acclaimed and influential rulings was a 1990 case balancing the rights of patients and the interests of medical researchers. A man sued doctors after an organ, removed during a life-saving operation, was tested and found to contain a cell pattern that was a potential source of new medical products. The court rejected the patient's claim of a violation of property rights, which could have entitled him to a share of the profits; but Panelli's majority opinion let him sue the doctor on more limited grounds, for failing to inform the patient of the research plans or obtain his consent. The ruling provided guidance to doctors and patients, left research unimpeded and discouraged the exploitation of unknowing patients.

But not all problems can be resolved so neatly. The court's tendency to create rigid categories, and its inclination to limit damage suits, have led it at times to try to pound square pegs into round holes. A glaring example involved assumption of risk, the doctrine that denies all damages to a person who engages in a dangerous activity and is injured by someone else's negligence. Most state courts have treated the concept as outdated since a 1975 state Supreme Court ruling that allowed damages when both parties were negligent, with the award reduced by the proportion of the victim's fault. But the Lucas court signaled in 1990 that it might revive the prohibition on damages, and granted review of about a dozen cases. Two years later, the court produced a fragmented and bewildering ruling.

In the case of a woman injured during a company football game, three justices, led by George, said sports participants had no duty to act carefully, and could be sued only for reckless or intentional harm. Three others, led by Kennard, said a suit should be allowed only if injuries resulted from activities that were more dangerous than the victim anticipated. The seventh justice, Mosk, said assumption of risk was outmoded, but agreed with George that no duty had been breached. Even the court couldn't figure out which of those standards to apply to the next case that raised the issue. The result, apparently, was that the approach of letting juries weigh the fault of each side had been discarded for dangerous activities, without any clearly defined policy to put in its place.

Further trouble lay ahead in a more significant case, involving suits for fear of disease caused by pollution. In the case of Salinas-area residents who learned their water wells had been contaminated with carcinogens, lower courts found their fears of cancer reasonable and awarded damages against the polluting company. But the Supreme Court, urged by businesses to prohibit all such suits and leery of "speculative fears," devised a new rule last December; In normal cases, damages would be awarded only if plaintiffs could prove they were more likely than not to become ill. But apparently unwilling to throw the Salinas residents out of court, the majority, led by Baxter, created an alternate test: They would have to prove only a significant risk of disease, because the polluter (according to the court) had disregarded a known risk of harm. The decision left the many interested parties on both sides neither satisfied nor enlightened. The new standards seemed arbitrary and the boundary lines murky. Underlying the decision may have been the court's unstated view that fears, like other emotions, are too intangible to be trusted as the basis of a lawsuit.

A similar approach outside the tort field resulted in perhaps the court's most awkward ruling in recent years — the December 1993 decision denying enforcement of Proposition 68, a 1988 campaign finance initiative.

Voters approved two political reform measures on the same ballot. Proposition 68, which included contribution limits as well as partial public financing for legislative candidates who limited their spending, got 53 percent of the vote. Proposition 73, which contained a different system

purpose of the initiative, said the four-member majority. Lucas' opinion said voters would have passed that provision by itself, even if they'd known in advance that the rest of the measure was invalid. What was left of Proposition 73 was still a competing regulatory scheme, and there was no room for Proposition 68, the court said.

The result was cheered by legislators and major contributors, but was hard to square with the court's professed reverence for the people's will. Two initiatives, both approved by a majority of the voters, had added up to zero reform. The ruling didn't even end the case; Proposition 73's legislative authors were soon back before the justices, asking for a new ruling that would rewrite their measure and cure its legal flaws.

The last few years have shown some weaknesses in the Lucas court, but the court is not without its strengths. It retains the support of much of the bench and bar, quickly mobilized behind Lucas when his travels came under scrutiny. It is also accepted by most of the public, which handily approved the current justices when they've appeared on the ballot, and is likely to do so again this fall. Despite a decline in the number of rulings, due largely to the increase in death penalty cases, the court is as hard-working as any of its predecessors. Lucas takes his leadership role seriously and has appointed productive task forces on racial and gender bias, technology, and the future of the court system. Mosk has been one of the nation's highest-regarded state judges for many years; the lesser-known Kennard and George appear to be extremely capable jurists with much untapped potential.

of contribution limits and several other provisions, including a ban on public financing, got 58 percent. The state Constitution says the ballot measure with the most votes prevails, but an appeals court, following some earlier appellate rulings, decided to allow enforcement of the parts of Proposition 68 that didn't conflict with Proposition 73. The Supreme Court disagreed and announced a new rule in 1990: When two ballot measure contain competing regulatory schemes, the measure with fewer voters is entirely unenforceable.

However, federal courts were already in the process of dismantling Proposition 73, and soon ruled that its core provision, the contribution limits, unconstitutionally favored incumbents. Proposition 68 had no such defect, so its sponsor, Common Cause, asked the state Supreme Court to revive the measure, since its rival had been effectively nullified. But the Supreme Court refused, and declared that Proposition 73 wasn't entirely dead; one previously obscure provision, broadening an existing ban on publicly financed mass political mailings, was unaffected by the federal rulings and was actually part of the essential

But the court, like a medieval royal family, suffers from inbreeding. For 12 years, two governors with a common agenda have promoted a succession of mostly like-minded justices from the appellate courts, with similar backgrounds as business or government lawyers, while stocking the lower courts with ex-prosecutors. When the high court justices sit around the conference table, there are no former poverty lawyers, civil-rights lawyers, labor lawyers, public defenders or academics, and probably few who have ever represented or have ever been, a poor person. That's not a formula for healthy debate. When the court hits a dead end in its thinking, it needs new ideas and new perspectives to find a way out.

Oddly enough, a possible prototype for change is sitting in the governor's office. When Wilson was a U.S. senator recommending candidates for federal judgeships, his picks were fairly diverse, racially, professionally and even ideologically. His appointments as governor have fit a different mold, but whoever is elected this November could strengthen the court by following Senator Wilson's model.

THE PRISON DILEMMA

California locks up more and more felons, so why don't we feel safer?

By Danielle Starkey and Vic Pollard

Reprinted from *California Journal*, April 1994

Adrian Raine's throat was slashed by a robber a few years ago. "I was furious. I was boiling. I wanted this guy put away forever,"Raine said recently.

But as a criminologist at the University of Southern California, Raine said he also recognized that locking up the robber and throwing away the key were not likely to reduce his chances of getting mugged in the future.

That Raine was mugged at all was, statistically speaking, a rare event. Despite the public's fear about crime, and the perception that it's getting worse, the state's overall crime rate has actually dropped since the peak year of 1980 in all except the violent-crime category. Much of the increase in violent crime is due to a reporting change because of legislation in 1986 that reclassified domestic violence from a misdemeanor to a felony.

Still, while statistics suggest that we should feel safer, few of us do. California's prison population has tripled since 1984, and the state spent more than $13 billion last year on its criminal justice system, which includes law enforcement, prosecution, probation, jails and prisons. Yet many people feel we're not doing enough, or the right things, to make a difference. Even if our chances of being murdered are about the same as dying of AIDS (.1 per 100,000), it's impossible to ignore, for example, that violent crime among juveniles is increasing at an alarming rate: The percentage of youths in the California Youth Authority for homicide went from 6.8 percent in 1987 to 12.1 percent in 1991.

But part of the problem is one of perception: News reports about a recent spate of particularly vicious, senseless crimes — most notably, the kidnap-murder of 12-year-old Polly Klaas — has made public safety a top political issue. Polls show that crime and violence have replaced the economy as the number-one concern among voters, resulting in a truckload of new legislation to crack down on criminals. California is one of at least 23 states considering proposals to sharply stiffen penalties for repeat offenders, usually labeled "three strikes and you're out." These measures differ in detail, but most are designed to impose longer sentences on people who have shown a propensity to commit repeated violent or serious offenses.

The new wave of anti-crime sentiment comes after more than a decade of increasingly stiffer penalties for many crimes. That has left much of the nation, especially California, with overcrowded prisons that consume an ever-growing share of scarce taxpayer dollars. Despite growing public fear and anger about crime, the question remains: Will locking up more criminals really make the streets safer?

Traditionally, the debate has been between two philosophies about human nature. There are those who say crime is a product of poverty, drugs or an abusive upbringing, and that vocational and educational programs could help turn around the lives of most offenders. And there are those who say that criminals are deviants who should be put away.

The debate is not new. In the 1920s and '30s, which included the bank-robbing heyday of Bonnie and Clyde, politicians were confronted with the same kind of demand for harsher penalties, said University of Minnesota law professor Michael Tonry. They reacted much the same way, passing harsh laws to crack down on what were then called "habitual offenders." But as prisons filled with increasingly elderly inmates like Robert Stroud, the famed "Bird Man of Alcatraz," a backlash set in during the 1950s and '60s. Rehabilitation advocates gained the upper hand, the death penalty became more controversial, and some states even granted wholesale pardons, Tonry said. The pendulum began swinging back the other way in the 1970s, as California and other states revived specific sentences for most crimes.

Back under California's old, indeterminate sentencing law (enacted in 1918), felons were sentenced to an open-ended term, such as five-years-to-life. Their actual release date was determined on a case-by-case basis by a state body called the

Adult Authority, which answered to no one and based its decisions on the inmates's crime and prison behavior.

"Under the indeterminate sentencing law, when you went to prison, you weren't quite sure when you were going to get out," said Bernie Orozco, a senior fiscal and policy analyst with the Legislative Analyst's Office. Further, there was a strong incentive to "be good" once you got out that doesn't exist today.

"It was a system to make sure that you were rehabilitated," said Orozco. "If by chance you did get out, and you acted up or had another incident, they could send you back [to prison] for the rest of your life."

The incentive apparently was effective. In 1975 only 11 percent of parolees were returned to prison for parole violations or for committing new crimes, according to the Little Hoover Commission, a watchdog agency of the executive branch of state government. By 1990, however, almost 80 percent of those released on parole were returned to prison for committing new crimes or violating the conditions of parole, although that rate has dropped to about 60 percent since then because the Department of Corrections has adopted a new policy of not sending back to prison many who violated terms of their parole.

The rapid rise in recidivism came in part as a result of the Determinate Sentencing Act of 1977, which essentially caused parole to fall by the wayside, and which itself grew out of complaints that indeterminate sentencing was subjective and racist. Even the California Supreme Court upheld a 1975 case that found that the Adult Authority didn't have standardized guidelines.

The act, which initially created finite sentences for each offense based on an average of time currently served for the crime, also "explicitly abandoned the long-standing purpose of prison as rehabilitation and instead established punishment as the state goal," according to a January 1994 report by the Little Hoover Commission — "Putting Violence Behind Bars: Redefining the Role of California's Prisons."

Since its enactment, piecemeal revisions of the law — usually following on the heels of a sensational crime — have resulted in a hodgepodge of sentencing requirements that one legal expert said "resembles the best offering of those who author bureaucratic memoranda, income tax forms, insurance policies or instructions for the assembly of packaged toys."

The repercussions of the law and its revisions have been extraordinary, and to some degree, unanticipated. "Every time there was a new crime that got media attention," sentencing requirements changed, said Jeannine English, executive director of the Little Hoover Commission. "There are people in prison for white-collar crimes serving sentences that are longer than for second-degree murderers, and burglary gets a longer sentence than taking corrosive acid and throwing it in someone's face."

In addition, inmates' release is no longer contingent on being able to show a means of support, or an evaluation of a successful transition back into society. For example, in the past year, 1022 inmates were released on parole from Pelican Bay, where most of the state's worst criminals are housed. Of these, 280 were released from the infamous "hole," or super-maximum security unit, where there are no efforts made to provide counseling, training or an education, and where inmates spend 22.5 hours per day in their cells.

"They're given $200 and dropped off at the Crescent City bus station," said English, of the Hoover Commission. One of these inmates took his cash, boarded a bus for the Bay Area and, within a month, had assaulted and raped a woman.

Another infamous parolee was multiple kidnapper Richard Allen Davis, charged in Polly Klaas's death. "All of the people who had worked with Richard Allen Davis, all of the people who knew him, *knew* he was going to continue his life of violence," said English. But he had served his time, so out he went.

"Our recommendation is that we keep violent offenders in prison until we're sure they're not going to be a threat, and

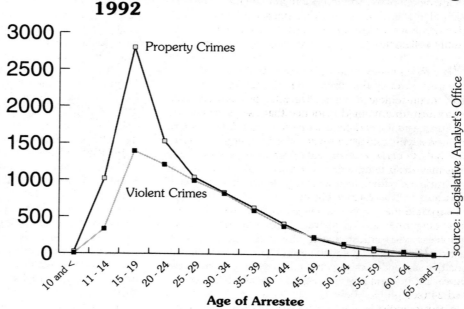

Felony Arrests Highest Among The Young[a]
1992

• Felony crime arrest rates peak in the 15- to 19-year-old age group.

• About half of all persons arrested in California in 1992 were between the ages of 11 and 24. This group, however, makes up only about 20 percent of the state's total population.

[a]Rate per 100,000 age-eligible population

source: Legislative Analyst's Office

to use other forms of punishment for non-violent offenders," said English. "That would be more cost-effective, and better for public safety, and create an opportunity to rehabilitate some of the non-violent offenders we deem could be rehabilitated."

In addition to giving indefinite sentences for violent criminals and habitual offenders, and restricting their ability to earn reduced sentence time, the Little Hoover Commission recommends lengthening the time beyond the present limitation of one year that a parolee can be returned to prison for a violent crime.

Yet lawmakers, and the public, remain enamoured of the three-strikes bills that would in fact incapacitate those who've committed crimes, but also would represent a multi-billion dollar investment in the back-end — and most expensive portion — of the state's criminal justice system. Assemblyman Phil Isenberg, a Sacramento Democrat, was one of the few legislators to try to stick out his hand to stop the locomotive, when he urged a "no" vote on the three-strikes bills before the Assembly. He said that, since he was elected in 1982, the prison population has gone from 28,000 to 120,000, and 10 prisons have been built, yet the public feels less secure than ever.

"You would think that if security is the goal, someone would step back and say, 'Wait a minute, if we tried higher penalties, greater enhancements, building more prisons, putting more people away and [we] still don't feel safe, then what's the answer?' Well, how about higher penalties, putting more people away, building more prisons, spending more... I mean, even a casual observer of the scene would say there's something screwy," Isenberg said.

Isenberg said one of the Legislature's goals should be to ensure that space in prison is available for violent offenders. Currently, 43 percent of all people in state prisons are there for violent crimes, and 57 percent are in for non-violent crimes. That's largely because local decision-makers naturally choose the least costly sentencing option from their perspective, and prison is free for them.

"Are we willing to say if we move non-violent people out of state prison that we ought to create alternative punishments for them? Hell no, we're not willing to say that. Why? Well, because somebody may put out an attack piece of mail that says you're soft on crime," Isenberg told his Assembly colleagues.

Criminal-justice experts are watching the "lock 'em up" frenzy with reactions ranging from sad bemusement to alarm. Decades of research have failed to turn up any solid evidence that longer sentences have been a significant deterrent on crime, RAND researcher Peter Greenwood told state senators considering the "three strikes" bills. Greenwood said certain offenses such as drunk driving may drop temporarily after penalties are stiffened due to a "shock" effect. "But whatever deterrent effect it has goes away in a year or two," he said.

Tonry said the chief reason is that most crimes, particularly violent crimes, are impulsive acts committed by people who don't stop to think about the consequences. Tonry and other experts also point out that the trend toward ever-longer mandatory sentences ignores the fact that the vast majority of crimes are committed by young men between the ages of 15 and 24 (see graph, page 33).

Except for individuals with serious mental illness, "There's huge amounts of evidence that the fires that burn inside people that cause them to commit violent crimes begin to burn out by the time they get to their 40s," Tonry said. "If you lock people up until they're in their 50s and 60s, all you're getting out of it is some temporary emotional satisfaction."

Increasing attention is also being paid to biological factors that appear to predispose people to violence, such as head injuries and birth complications, although the conclusions are still speculative and controversial.

So how can the state fashion a corrections policy that keeps violent offenders off the streets and does not eat up money needed for other public programs? There are some examples of systems that work well, experts say. Minnesota and Delaware are credited with creating some of the best models in the 1980s. They rejected both mandatory sentences for all crimes and indeterminate sentences, in which parole decisions are usually made on a case-by-case basis by gubernatorial appointees. Instead, they set up independent agencies that established sentencing guidelines that take into account a wide variety of factors in each individual case, such as the seriousness of the crime and the likelihood of repeat offenses.

Since Delaware's guidelines went into effect in 1987, it has seen a marked increase in incarceration for violent crimes, while incarceration for non-violent offenses has dropped by almost half and its prison population has even declined slightly, according to the National Conference of State Legislatures. Experts caution that such a system must be coupled with an effective probation and parole supervision system, programs that have been increasingly starved for money in California in recent years. They also warn against adopting a system that is too complicated to administer fairly, the chief complaint about the controversial guidelines of the federal judicial system.

California's Legislative Analyst's Office recommended last year in its booklet, "Making Government Make Sense," that the state work more closely with local governments to decide how to best utilize each other's resources. "The way it's set up now, they're each trying to shunt off workloads on each other," said Orozco. In other words, since local governments can send people to prison at no charge, that's exactly what they choose to do, even though it costs more to taxpayers.

"The [local governments] should determine the length of the sentence, and they should pay for the service" through a revenue-redistribution plan, said Craig Cornett, director of criminal justice and state administration for the LAO. "We think that changes the fiscal incentives in a really positive way, and among other things encourages them to do more at the front end for prevention in order to prevent that back end cost."

In addition, Cornett said, a blue-ribbon commission convened in 1990 on inmate population management produced a comprehensive, balanced study that has largely been ignored.

"The key conclusion they had was that the system is out of balance, which we think is completely true," Cornett said. "We have too many resources at the back end, and not enough at the middle or at the beginning. We especially don't have enough at the front end to prevent people from becoming defendants or to deal with them when they first

Crime Rate Remains Stable Despite Sharp Increase in Imprisonment[a]
1971 Through 1992

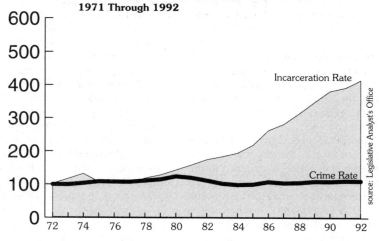

Incarceration Rate

Crime Rate

source: Legislative Analyst's Office

[a] Change in rates per 100,000 population, indexed to 1972

- California's incarceration rate has increased almost 300 percent since 1971 while the crime rate remained relatively flat (it increased about 11 percent).

- Some reasearchers argue that this situation should be expected because they believe that incarcerating more people for a longer period of time has no impact on the crime rate. Others disagree and argue that the crime rate would have increased significantly if the rate of imprisonment had not increased so significantly.

enter the system, but we put a lot of resources in the back end to warehouse people in state prison after they've committed the crime."

Nevertheless, it's likely that's exactly where money is going to go, given the momentum of the "three strikes" solution. Governor Pete Wilson's administration, in what it acknowledged is a conservative estimate, predicted recently that the proposed "three strikes" initiative would require construction of 20 new prisons by the turn of the century — in addition to the 12 new facilities expected to be needed under current sentencing laws. They would cost $2 billion a

year to operate. Prison operating costs would continue to increase for the first 30 years under the program, maxing out at $5.7 billion a year by 2027.

These numbers didn't seem to deter lawmakers, however; during the first week of March, a bill identical to the "three strikes" initiative breezed out of the Legislature and was signed by Governor Wilson. Alternative bills, designed to address other problems as well as get tough on violent criminals, stalled. During the second week of March, proponents of the "three strikes" initiative turned in signatures to get their measure on the ballot. 🏛

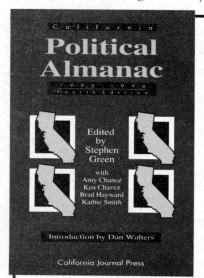

California
Political Almanac
1995–1996
Fourth Edition

Edited by Stephen Green

with
Amy Chance
Ken Chavez
Brad Hayward
Kathie Smith

Introduction by Dan Walters

California Journal Press

New!
California Political Almanac
1995-96

Every reader becomes a political insider with this candid analysis of California's political leaders written by Sacramento's most knowledgeable journalists. The new 1995-96 edition is now available.

Biographies, photographs, voting records and district descriptions for every member of the state Senate, Assembly and Congress. Chapters on the bureaucracy, lobbyists, media, local government : 550 pages of data and analysis.

Price $34.95

Special offer: 1993-94 edition reduced to $17.45 alone or $9.95 with 1995-96 edition.

◆

Please add 7.75% sales tax plus $2.75 handling to each order. Use the handy insert card to place orders.
Or just write your own and send it with payment (American Express, VISA or Master Card orders accepted) to
California Journal, 2101 K Street, Sacramento, CA 95816
or call ◆ 916/444-2840 ◆ Fax 916/446-5369

THE LEGISLATURE

California's Legislature is not much different from Congress and legislative bodies in other states in overall power and structure. It is, simply stated, the policy-making arm of government, restricted only by the federal and state constitutions and the governor's veto. Like Congress, it can also conduct investigations into almost any issue of public concern and impeach public officials. The Senate must ratify top-level, non-judicial appointments of the governor, while both houses have the opportunity to reject the executive's nominations for any vacancy among the state's constitutional offices. It also can ratify amendments to the United States Constitution. In recent years, there has been a trend toward the Legislature's appropriating for itself some of the appointive power traditionally given to the executive. Thus, it is not uncommon now to have a commission consist of both gubernatorial and legislative appointees.

Seats in both the 40-member Senate and 80-member Assembly are apportioned on the basis of population and under the 1991 reapportionment for the first time the court joined two adjacent assembly districts into one senate district throughout the state. (Until 1966, the Senate was apportioned by geography, like the United States Senate.) Assembly members serve two-year terms; Senate terms are for four years, with half the terms expiring every two years. Under the provisions of Prop. 140 of November 1990, term limits are now imposed on state legislators (3 terms, 6 years in the Assembly; 2 terms, 8 years in the Senate). The Senate and Assembly are organized differently, with power diffused in a committee of the upper house but centered in the office of speaker in the Assembly.

The Senate

The lieutenant governor is the president of the Senate, but this official has virtually no power. The lieutenant governor is entitled to cast a vote to break a 20-20 tie, but this is very rare. If the Senate can be said to have a single leader it is the president pro tempore, who is elected by a simple majority of his colleagues. The pro tem is charged with overall administration of the house, but the real power — committee appointments and assignment of bills to committee — rests with the five-member Rules Committee. The president pro tempore is chairman, and the other four seats are traditionally divided between the two major parties. In the past rural vs. urban, north vs. south or personal animosities created conflict. In recent years the divisions in the Senate have tended to be along party lines. David Roberti provided stable leadership to the Senate from 1980 (when Willie Brown was elected speaker) to 1994 when Roberti was forced to leave the Senate because of term limits, the first state legislator in the nation to be forced out of office. The current President pro Tempore is Senator Bill Lockyer.

Aside from the Rules Committee, the two most important panels in the Senate are the Appropriations and Budget and Fiscal Review committees. The Budget and Fiscal Review Committee handles the budget. The Appropriations Committee hears any other bills with direct or implied state cost. Thus it can kill almost any major bill.

The Assembly

Until 1995 the Assembly had a form of government that might be called self-inflicted dictatorship. The speaker was elected by at least 41 votes (a simple majority) and thereafter wielded tremendous power; this officer appointed all committee chairs and named all committee members except for the Rules Committee. Control over committees amounted to the power to kill any bill. A bill defeated in committee could be brought to the floor by a majority vote of the full assembly, but this occured very infrequently. A vote to withdraw a bill from committee would be tantamount to a vote of no-confidence for the speaker. The speaker's control over legislation made whoever holds this office the second-most-powerful official in state government next to the governor. However, on occasion, the speaker had difficulty leading. Battles within majority Democratic ranks in 1979-80 between then-Speaker Leo McCarthy and challenger Howard Berman, each with his own faction, led to legislative paralysis in the lower house. In 1988 the "Gang of Five" (anti-leadership Democrats) openly feuded with Democratic Speaker Willie Brown over legislative matters in the Assembly. Though the five were punished by Speaker Brown (losing chairmanships, committee assignments, staff and office space) they refused to back down. For a time, the "Five" combined with the Republican caucus had a majority in the Assembly. However after the November 1988 elections, Democrats had 42 seats plus the rebellious "Gang of Five" who were no longer needed for a majority. The "Five" returned to the Democratic fold, and their transgressions forgiven.

However, a combination of term-limits-fomented-bailouts of veteran Democractic assembly members, the court-designed reapportionment of 1991, and a nationwide Republican surge provided the necessary ingredients for substantial Republican gains and corresponding Democratic losses in the Assembly in the 1994 general election. After the dust settled, 41 Republicans and 39 Democrats were elected to the Assembly. Many pundits began writing Willie Brown's epitaph as speaker. It appeared that Brown would lose his speakership and that Republican leader Jim Brulte would replace him. However, it didn't happen—then. Rumors of Willie Brown's political death were exaggerated: Brown had an ace up his sleeve. Republican Assembly member Paul Horcher switched from Republican ranks to independent in early December 1994. On the floor he surprised his GOP brethren by voting for Willie Brown as speaker. This created a 40-40 tie and meant there was no immediate resolution of the leadership issue for the time being. Horcher said he left Republican ranks because Republican assembly leadership had become too conservative (and had shunned him for being to cooperative with the Democrats).

In January, Democrats and Horcher moved to oust Republican Richard Mountjoy from the Assembly. Mountjoy had been elected simultaneously to the Assembly and to the Senate in a special election in the 1994 election. Although Mountjoy fought to stay in the Assembly so that he could continue to vote for Brulte, he was removed in mid-January 1995 on a 40-39 vote. (Of course, if he had resigned from his Senate seat, he could have remained in the Assembly.) With

Mountjoy gone, Willie Brown was elected as speaker 40-39 (not with the customary 41-vote margin).

Because of the unique circumstances in his speakership election and the even balance of Republican-Democrat strength in the Assembly, Speaker Brown and Democrats established a power-sharing arrangement with Republicans. Of 26 standing committees, 13 are chaired by Democrats picked by Brown and 13 are chaired by Republicans picked by Brulte. Brown and Brulte also selected their own party colleagues to the various committees with all committees having equal numbers of Republicans and Democrats.

Meanwhile, Republicans, angered by Horcher's action launched and qualified a recall against the GOP turncoat. In addition, at least one other recall effort was undertaken by GOP forces against Democrat Mike Machado in a marginal district in the Central Valley. Given the fact that some Assembly members may be resigning their seats in mid-term to run for other offices (including Willie Brown), the recalls, and feisty members (Republican Doris Allen has threatened not to vote for Brulte because several of her bills were killed by GOP members), predicting future speakers is hazardous.

In any case, instability and turmoil will likely be the pattern in the Assembly for the forseeable future. Every two years a fresh new wave of 30-35 rookie legislators will be elected. The grizzled veterans will be members who have served for a term or two. One thing is certain however: the immense power speakers such as Willie Brown once held is a relic of the past. Post-Brown speakers may retain the traditional legislative powers of the speaker, but will not be able to exert the all-encompassing influence of the past in the new term limits era.

Much of Willie Brown's power hinged on continuity (he's now in his 15th year as speaker and 31st as Assembly member.); his ability to maintain the Democratic majority; and his success in wheedling large campaign donations from special interests (concerned about what passed or what was killed in the Assembly) and then divvying them out to Democratic Assembly members for their campaigns. This is gone. In the new term-limits era the Assembly Rules Committee may become more important in the Assembly in performing its various housekeeping duties: assigning bills to committee, setting salaries for legislative employees, determining offices for members and purchasing supplies. The Senate is likely to become the more influential legislative house because the upper house will have more experienced members. After all, most new senators have previously served in the Assembly. In the new term limits era, it is also possible that some term-limited senators may be able to continue their political careers by running for the Assembly (if they haven't already served six years there after 1990).

Legislation

There are three basic types of legislation: bills, constitutional amendments and resolutions. These measures can only be introduced by legislators. The governor cannot introduce a bill, but he can ask a friendly member to put it in the hopper. Even the governor's budget carries the name of a lawmaker. In fact, however, very few bills are the direct inspiration of a legislator. Most bills come from interest groups, staff members, constituents, government officials, or a variety of other sources.

A bill is simply a proposed statute. It can be enacted by a simple majority vote in both houses unless it is an urgency measure or carries an appropriation, in which case a two-thirds vote of approval is required. Constitutional amendments are proposed changes to the state Constitution; a two-thirds vote of each house will place one of these measures on the ballot for voter consideration. Resolutions are merely statements of legislative viewpoint. They may be addressed to other governmental agencies, describe state general policy, or commend or memorialize someone. They are normally passed by voice vote. Constitutional amendments and resolutions, unlike bills, are not subject to gubernatorial veto.

Legislative process

When a member introduces a bill, its title is read and it is printed. Then it is assigned to a committee by the Assembly or Senate Rules Committee. The committee hearing is the most crucial stage in the legislative process, for it is at this point — not on the floor — that the fate of most legislation is determined. Following public hearing, the committee can kill the measure or send it to another committee (usually the fiscal committee) or to the floor as is or with recommended amendments. When it reaches the floor, the bill's title is read a second time, amendments are often made, and the legislation is placed on the agenda for debate. After debate, a roll call is taken. If the bill is passed, it is sent to the other house, where the same process takes place. If the bill is amended in the second house, it must return to the house of origin for acceptance or rejection of the amendments. If approved at this point, the bill goes to the governor for signature or veto. If the amendments are rejected, a conference committee of three members of each house is formed to compromise differences. This procedure is always followed on the budget and often used at the end of a session to speed the last-minute rush of bills (because a conference committee report can be produced more rapidly than a revised printed version of a bill).

A bill goes to the governor if both houses approve a conference committee recommendation.

In the Senate, roll calls are taken orally by the secretary of the Senate and aides. Once a roll call is concluded, members may not change their votes, and absent members cannot add their votes. The Assembly uses an electronic vote counter. Members push switches, and lights shine on a board — green reflecting aye; red, no. With the unanimous consent of the membership, members are allowed to change their votes the same day or add their votes if their actions do not alter the outcome.

Legislative modernization

Until 1966, the Legislature met for general sessions in odd-numbered years and for short budget sessions in even-numbered years. Legislators then received $6,000 a year, and their elective positions were not considered to be full-time occupations. In 1966, the voters approved Proposition 1a making each year's session unlimited, raising the pay to $16,000 and allowing lawmakers to give themselves cost-of-living increases of five percent a year. In the June 1990 primary election voters approved Prop. 112. While some of the provisions of this constitutional amendment established new ethics regulations, perhaps its key feature was the creation of a new Citizens' Compensation Commission. The reason this amendment was proposed was because the Legislature angered many votes when they voted to increase their salaries. To deflect this criticism the commission was established. In December 1991 the new commission raised salaries of state legislators from $40,816 a year to $52,500. In addition, legislative leaders received extra compensation. Current salaries established by the commission are: legislator, $75,600; Speaker and President pro Tem, $90,720, and floor leaders, $83,160.

In 1972, the people approved another constitutional amendment. This one put the Legislature on the same two-year schedule as Congress, with bills remaining alive for two years. The Legislature now is in session year-round, with breaks for Easter, Christmas, part of the summer and during statewide elections. In addition to their salaries, legislators receive $109 a day for expenses and have use of leased automobiles, credit cards and district offices.

In addition to the standing committees, which consider the merits of bills, the Legislature also establishes two-house joint committees and one-house select committees to study specific problems (often of special concern to only one legislator, who becomes chairman of the committee). These committees can submit recommendations to the Legislature but have no direct power over legislation. Many of these select committees have been eliminated under the new budget strictures of Proposition 140.

Legislative staff

Each member of the Legislature has a personal staff plus the assistance of specialists assigned to committees and to the party caucuses. There are also three major independent bureaus with significant influence on the legislative process— the legislative counsel, the legislative analyst, and the auditor general.

• *Legislative counsel*, Bion Gregory, has a large staff of attorneys to provide legal advice to lawmakers and draft their bills and proposed amendments.

• *Legislative analyst*, Elizabeth Hill, provides advice to the Legislature on anything with a fiscal implication, which can cover virtually every major bill. The analyst annually publishes a detailed analysis of the governor's budget, which becomes the basis for legislative hearings on the fiscal program.

• *Auditor general*, Kurt R. Sjoberg, conducts investigations of state agencies to determine whether they can be run more economically and efficiently, he reports directly to the Joint Audit Committee and to the Legislature as a whole.

In all, a staff of some 2,000 served the Legislature until the passage of Prop. 140 in November 1990 which mandated term limits for members and budget reductions for the Legislature. The Legislature's staff has been reduced to comply with the measure. In addition to the analyst, auditor general, and counsel, there are sergeants-at-arms, secretaries, political aides, and committee consultants. The consultants are the most important element of the staff; they provide specialized knowledge for committees, gather information and provide independent evaluation of information obtained from interest groups, the governor and others.

Reapportionment

Almost nothing stirs the juices of a legislator — either at the state or federal level — as much as the prospect of his or her district being reapportioned. Redistricting takes place every decade and has the potential of throwing many legislators out of office. Every congressional, Senate and Assembly district in California must be redrawn after each census to ensure districts are equal in population.

California's Assembly districts have always been apportioned by population, but the state Senate has been apportioned under two systems. Prior to 1926, the Senate was also apportioned by population, but in that year the voters approved a "federal plan" devised by Northern Californians to keep control of the Senate from rapidly growing Southern California. This plan provided that no county could have more than one senator and that one senator could represent no more than three counties. As a result, the senator from Los Angeles at one time represented 440 times more people than the senator from Alpine, Inyo and Mono counties. This was the most severe apportionment imbalance in the nation. Such discrepancies were eradicated in 1966, when the U.S. Supreme Court's "one-man, one-vote" edict went into effect.

Redistricting can be simple if both houses of a legislature and the governor are of the same political party. The party in power merely divides the state to suit itself and gives the opposition party the scraps. The usual procedure is to offer some members of the opposition good deals so that a nominally bipartisan reapportionment bill can be passed. Actually, it is impossible to create good districts for one party without fashioning some just as good for the other. But the legislators doing the redistricting can usually pick and choose whom to favor among members of the opposition. In the 1980's reapportionment, although Democrat Jerry Brown was governor and Democrats had solid majorities in both houses, Republicans stymied the majority party's reapportionment plans by qualifying three separate referenda for the June 1982 ballot. Voters voted "no" against the three Democratic sponsored bills and forced the Democrats to make some adjustments to the district lines.

Under the state Constitution, the Legislature is empowered to reapportion all seats (52 in Congress, 40 Senate and 80 Assembly districts), subject only to a gubernatorial veto. Thus, when a governor is of a different party than the Legislature's leadership an impasse is apt to develop. In this case, either a bi-partisan plan is drawn favoring the incumbents of both parties, maintaining the status quo, or the matter ends up in the courts.

Republicans tried repeatedly in the 1980s to modify the reapportioning process. Their objective was to shift the decision making away from Democratic legislative leaders:

1) In 1982 Republicans joined with Common Cause and qualified Prop. 14 to establish an independent districting commission to do the reapportioning. Voters defeated the proposal.

2) In 1983 then Assemblyman Don Sebastiani qualified a new initiative which provided, he claimed, "fairer" districts than the one the Democrats had devised. This initiative was declared unconstitutional by the state Supreme Court prior to its being voted upon. The court ruled that reapportioning could take place only once each decade.

3) In 1984 Governor Deukmejian authored an initiative to have reapportioning handled by a panel of retired appellate judges. Voters rejected this proposal.

The 1991 reapportionment plans passed by the Democratic-controlled Legislature were vetoed by Republican Governor Pete Wilson. Because of the impasse, districts were drawn by the state Supreme Court with the help of "special masters." 🏛

CALIFORNIA'S LEGISLATIVE PROCESS

INITIAL STEPS BY AUTHOR

IDEA

Sources of bills: legislators, legislative committees, governor, state and local governmental agencies, business firms, lobbyists, citizens.

DRAFTING

Formal copy of bill and "layman's digest" prepared by Legislative Counsel.

INTRODUCTION

Bill submitted by senator or Assembly member. Numbered and read first time. Referred to policy committee by Assembly or Senate Rules Committee. Printed.

ACTION IN HOUSE OF ORIGIN

COMMITTEE

Testimony taken from author, proponents and opponents. Typical actions: Do pass; amend and do pass; no action; hold in committee (kill); amend and re-refer to same committee; refer to another committee; send to interim study.

Bills with any fiscal implications, if approved by policy committee, are referred to Appropriations Committee in the Senate and to Ways and Means Committee in the Assembly.

SECOND READING

Bills given do-pass recommendations are read the second time and placed on the daily file (agenda) for debate on a subsequent day.

FLOOR DEBATE AND VOTE

Bills are read the third time and debated. A roll-call vote follows. For ordinary bills, 21 votes are needed in the Senate and 41 in the Assembly. For urgency bills and most appropriations measures, 27 and 54 votes are required. If these numbers are not reached, the bill is defeated. Any member may seek reconsideration and a second vote. If passed or passed with amendments, the bill is sent to the second house.

ACTION IN SECOND HOUSE

READING

Bill is read the first time and referred to committee by the Assembly or Senate Rules Committee.

COMMITTEE

Procedures and possible actions are nearly identical to those in the first house.

SECOND READING

If cleared by committee, the bill is read a second time and placed on the daily file (agenda) for debate and vote.

FLOOR DEBATE AND VOTE

The procedure is identical to the first house. If a bill is passed without having been amended in the second house, it is sent to the governor's desk. (Resolutions are sent to the secretary of state's office.) If amended in the second house and passed, the measure returns to the house of origin for consideration of amendments.

RESOLUTION OF TWO-HOUSE DIFFERENCES (IF NECESSARY)

CONCURRENCE

The house of origin decides whether to accept the second-house amendments. If the amendments are approved, the bill is sent to the governor. If the amendments are rejected, the bill is placed in the hands of a two-house conference committee composed of three senators and three Assembly members.

CONFERENCE

If the conferees fail to agree, the bill dies. If the conferees present a recommendation for compromise (conference report), both houses vote on the report. If the report is adopted by both, the bill goes to the governor. If either house rejects the report, a second (and even a third) conference committee may be formed.

THE GOVERNOR

SIGN OR VETO?

Within 12 days after receiving a bill, the governor may sign it into law, allow it to become law without his signature or veto it. Bill is sent to Secretary of State's office and given a chapter number. A vetoed bill returns to the house of origin for possible vote on overriding the veto. It requires a two-thirds majority of both houses to override. Urgency measures may become effective immediately after signing. Others usually take effect the following January 1st.

Copyright 1995 Information for Public Affairs, Inc.

The Legacy of the Capitol Sting

After 14 convictions and guilty pleas, it's business as usual in the Legislature's fantasy land

by Steve Scott

Reprinted from *California Journal*, August 1994

Photos by Rich Pedroncelli

Former Senator Joseph Montoya

On the last night of the 1988 legislative session, it seemed the most popular gathering spot in Sacramento was the desk of Assemblyman Lloyd Connelly. A steady stream of members of both parties sauntered over to the southeast corner of the chamber, where the Sacramento Democrat sat, asking his advice or just making conversation. Now Connelly was hardly a power broker: he chaired no committees, raised relatively little money, and was considered at the time to be among the worst-dressed members of the Legislature. Yet his computer-generated "bad bills list" was suddenly the most sought-after piece of paper in the Capitol.

"For awhile there, every time I voted 'no', 15 to 20 red lights would immediately go up," Connelly, who is now a judge, chuckles in recollection.

Why was there such a sudden interest in Connelly's little "no" list? Because on two different occasions, it included legislation crafted to give a tax break to an obscure shrimp-packing company trying to locate in West Sacramento. A week earlier, it had been revealed that the legislation had been planted by the FBI as part of an undercover sting that had ended with a late-night raid on four legislative offices at the Capitol. That Connelly was the only member of the Assembly to vote against the FBI bill twice speaks to his own studiousness and attention to detail. The swiftness by which he was transformed into the lighthouse guiding his colleagues through special-interest waters speaks to what many consider the situational ethics of the Legislature as an institution: Without a strong Magnetic North, the moral compass spins to fit the circumstances.

It's been six years since the aforementioned raid at the Capitol, and eight years since the FBI began its undercover probe into corruption in the Legislature. The scorecard of convictions is not a happy one for the state's institutions of government: five sitting or former members of the Legislature; five former staffers; a member of the California Coastal

Commission; one of the Capitol's most powerful lobbyists; and Yolo County's top two law-enforcement officials. While six copped pleas, eight of the 14 were found guilty by juries of ordinary citizens from Sacramento and its environs, all of which reached their verdicts with amazing swiftness. Yet, despite eight years of having their institution tarnished by the stain of corruption and perceived avarice, many within the Capitol's cloistered confines have responded merely by pointing fingers: at the federal prosecutors, at the media, at the jurors, at the voters, at "the system." Everywhere but at their own hearts.

The five-year chronology of the operation codenamed "Brispec" (for "Bribery/Special Interest") is familiar to most whose jobs are intertwined with the Legislature. In early 1986 FBI agent John Brennan began posing as an Alabama businessman looking to build a shrimp-processing plant in West Sacramento. Wearing a wire, "Jack Gordon" began looking for corners in which to lay the trap. The trail led first to John Shahabian, a big-talking Senate Rules staffer who operated more

Former Coastal Commissioner Mark Nathanson (center).

or less without portfolio. Shahabian's ham-handed shakedowns made him an easy mark, and when the feds showed him what they had, he agreed to become a government informant and the web grew.

The world learned of Brispec on a warm Sacramento night in August 1988, when an army of FBI agents raided a number of legislative offices at the state Capitol, searching for evidence. Among those targeted in the raids were state Senator Alan Robbins (D-Van Nuys), Assembly members Frank Hill (R-Whittier) and Gwen Moore (D-Los Angeles), and Assembly Republican Leader Pat Nolan (R-Glendale). The cloud hoisted over the Capitol as a result of that all-night raid grew darker and more ominous as the years rolled by. The procession of convictions began with the February 1990 guilty verdict against Senator Joseph Montoya (D-Whittier) on seven counts of racketeering, extortion and conspiracy. Later that year, former Senator Paul Carpenter (D-Los Angeles), who ran the Senate Democrats' political fund-raising arm, was convicted on corruption charges. The next year brought convictions of former legislative staffers Tyrone Netters and Daryl Freeman and a guilty plea from Robbins. For a year prior to his guilty plea, Robbins had been acting as a government informant, and his testimony helped take down two more defendants, former Coastal Commissioner Mark Nathanson (who pleaded guilty) and high-powered lobbyist Clay Jackson (convicted in December of last year). The Jackson

case also produced a second conviction for Carpenter, who skipped the country before his scheduled sentencing and now is facing extradition from Costa Rica.

When 1994 dawned, only Hill — since elected to the state Senate — and Nolan remained unprosecuted. Both had been among the group whose offices were raided in 1988. Nolan opted to plead guilty in February rather than face trial, but Hill decided to tough it out. Like Montoya in the first of the Brispec trials, Hill was convicted largely on the strength of videotapes showing him receiving a $2500 honorarium from another undercover agent. Prosecutors said that, in the tape, Hill looked "like an employee reporting to [his] boss." Hill's lawyer, Stephen Miller, insisted his client "never believed he was taking any official action in return for the honorarium." But while Hill may not have believed it was a *quid pro quo*, the jury did, taking less than nine hours to find him guilty on all three counts against him. The book on Brispec was finally closed.

If any other institution had been subjected to such a clean sweep of prosecutions and convictions, the consequences would have been profound for its leadership. In the business world, such an event would send stock tumbling, stir up revolution among shareholders, and cause just about every head in upper management to roll. Local school board members tainted by this kind of scandal couldn't leave their houses without bumping into someone carrying a recall petition against them. Even in the executive branches of government, scandal at this level could bring down a president or governor. In the Legislature, however, the response can largely be summed up in one word: denial.

"I don't think Hill did anything wrong," says Senate

Republican Leader Ken Maddy of Fresno. "I don't agree with the verdict."

"It is impossible in this atmosphere to overcome the almost innate handicap of any governmental official tried before Sacramento juries," says Senator Quentin Kopp (I-San Francisco).

"The fact is that honoraria were legal," says former Assemblywoman Bev Hansen (R-Santa Rosa) of the payoff that resulted in Hill's conviction. "[Hill] is taking a fall because the public believes that politicians are crooks."

Several who didn't have any direct comment on the verdicts themselves insisted the prosecutions were merely cases of people who went overboard getting caught. "Every institution has a few bad apples," said Senate President pro Tem Bill Lockyer (D-Hayward). "In our case, they've been turned into apple sauce."

To suggest that the federal probe has had no effect on legislative attitudes toward ethics would be untrue. Even critics of the Legislature concede the scrutiny of prosecutors has made lawmakers more careful in their dealings with lobbyists and others who contribute to their campaigns. "Their level of awareness has been raised considerably regarding the public perception of what they do," says Ruth

Former Senator Paul Carpenter (center).

Holton, executive director of California Common Cause. "In their dealings with lobbyists, they are more careful not to imply a connection with what they do." One lawmaker even went so far as to include an admonition against any implied *quid pro quo* in a fund-raising letter he sent to potential contributors.

"I think there has been a chilling effect on some of the activity of some of the members," admits Assembly Speaker Willie Brown Jr. (D-San Francisco).

There also have been institutional reforms. The Montoya conviction spurred passage of a constitutional amendment that became Proposition 112. The measure, approved by voters in November 1990, banned honoraria — essentially a check that goes straight into the lawmaker's pocket —

entirely, and severely limited gifts. It also established stricter ethical guidelines for lawmakers, including a requirement that they take an ethics training course every year. "In 1988 there was no clear line with respect to honoraria," says Kopp. "If honoraria had been outlawed, we wouldn't be having such a discussion today."

Still, it is remarkable how little has actually changed since 1988. Two of the four legislative leaders in place at the time of the raid — Maddy and Brown — remain in their posts. A third, then-Senate President pro Tem David Roberti, remained in his post until early this year, when he stepped aside to run for treasurer. Only Nolan's early ouster as Assembly GOP leader can be connected with the fallout from Brispec, and even then his removal had as much to do with his caucus losing elections as it did with the scandal itself. Moreover, the biggest changes to the institution have come not as a result of self-correction, but rather as an outgrowth of voter dissatisfaction. The impact of Proposition 140, the term-limit initiative, dwarfs anything Proposition 112 might have done to reform the Legislature.

Also unchanged is the attitudes of many lawmakers about their fund-raising habits. The vast majority of lawmakers — be they Republican or Democrat; veteran or newcomer — continue to scoop up hundreds of thousands of dollars in contributions from lawyers, doctors, insurance companies, tobacco companies, teachers unions, prison guard unions, corporations and consortiums, all the while insisting these contributions have no effect on the way they vote, or how they conduct themselves in their jobs. When a reporter suggested to Lockyer recently that *quid pro quo* arrangements might be continuing, Lockyer tersely responded, "Prove it." To the extent that Brispec has had an impact, he insists, it has been merely to weed out a few bad apples who obviously went over the line. "Inappropriate behavior has been cut off, and I would anticipate that to become part of the culture," he says.

"When an issue comes up, do you pay attention to [contributors]? Yes, you pay attention to them," says Assemblyman Phil Isenberg (D-Sacramento). "But if you don't have the courage of your convictions, you shouldn't be in the business."

Isenberg's words echo the somewhat saltier manifesto of the late Assembly Speaker Jesse Unruh, who suggested that if a legislator couldn't accept the sundry pleasures offered by lobbyists and still vote against them, they didn't belong in the Legislature. For many outside the manicured grounds of Capitol Park, however, these bromides don't pass the "giggle test."

"If somebody gives you enough money over a period of time, naturally you're going to vote the way they want you to," said Robert Bartosh, a juror in the Clay Jackson trial. "The system allows it to happen."

"You can convince yourself, I suppose, that being contributed to doesn't influence you," says political scientist Sherry Bebitch-Jeffe, who used to work for Unruh. "I don't see that there's any way it cannot."

That pressure doesn't just come from the lobbyists or contributors — it sometimes comes from within the institution itself. While in the Assembly, Connelly eschewed social contact with lobbyists, and avoided inviting advocates to fund raisers, calling the practice "morally corrosive." As a result, he was routinely among the five worst fund raisers among Assembly Democrats. His reward for this attention to appearances? A decade in the Assembly, zero committee chairmanships. Yet even Connelly felt the heat from his donors when an issue came up and they wanted his vote.

"I've been there, and it's actual pressure," he says. "Unless there's a conscious effort to separate yourself from that kind of inducement, I think the average person can get trapped."

The ease with which even reasonably honest people can get sucked into an ethical gray zone suggests to many that the main lesson to be learned from Brispec is that the campaign-finance system is a failure. "We're looking at a fall campaign where you could see spending of $200 million," says Larry Berg, director of the Jesse Unruh Institute of Politics. "That's a lot of money, and it's got to come from somewhere." Common Cause's Holton says "it's not the individuals, it's the system, and until the system is cleaned up, we're going to continue to have this kind of problem."

The problem, of course, is that campaign reform means different things to different people. Holton, Berg, and any number of others believe the best way to "clean up" the system is to institute campaign spending limits and public financing of legislative elections. By replacing privately raised contributions with public money, they argue, legislators would be obliged to consider the views of ordinary citizens at least as much as those of large contributors.

"The taxpayers are being pennywise and pound-foolish in not doing this," says Berg. "This would remove the cloud over elections and the process." For many in both parties, however, the notion of using taxpayers' money to finance elections is a political non-starter.

"There's no indication that California taxpayers are willing to spend a dime on politicians right now," says attorney Joe Remcho, who has represented the Legislature in

Former lobbyist Clay Jackson (left)

court battles over campaign reform.

These differing views of campaign reform are often less driven by ideology than by partisan advantage. This year, legislation that would institute public financing of legislative campaigns cleared the Assembly Elections and Reapportionment Committee, the furthest such legislation has gotten. However, the bill, authored by Lockyer, contains very broad contribution limits and allows virtually unfettered transfers from legislative caucus PACs to candidates — a position which advantages Democrats. On the other side, 1988's Proposition 73, which the state Supreme Court has recently agreed to re-hear, imposes only contribution limits and bans transfers among candidates — a position which advantages Republicans. With this level of partisan conniving, it's little wonder reform efforts are hardly moving at light speed.

Ultimately, however, any discussion about ethics must go beyond a mere consideration of legal construction, for questions about ethics are, at their core, questions about conscience. "You don't just legislate ethical issues out of existence," says Alan Rosenthal, director of the Eagleton Institute on Politics at Rutgers University. "The legislative community needs to take responsibility for training and guiding members, and good examples need to be set by leadership." Bebitch-Jeffe believes it is an ethics vacuum at the top that has brought the California Legislature to its current state. "There's no leader saying, 'Let's clean house and get it together,'" she laments. "There is tinkering around the margins, but people don't trust the solutions that come out of the institution."

To reverse this trend, Bebitch-Jeffe, Rosenthal and others say lawmakers should take the perception of impropriety every bit as seriously as they take the law itself. "The message ought to be that commonly accepted ethical standards ought to kick in, even where the law doesn't prohibit something," says attorney Remcho. Connelly offers his former colleagues a simpler admonition: "Just call 'em straight," he says. "It's good government, and I believe it's good politics." The extent to which lawmakers follow Connelly's advice will likely be the extent to which the "Shrimpgate" scandal leaves a lasting imprint on the Capitol.

"For those who care about our political institutions, these scandals should be wake-up calls," says Rosenthal. "I'm sorry many legislators haven't awakened, but I guess some of them are very heavy sleepers." 🏛

Legislative staff

Coping with term limits and an unstable job market

Illustration by Christopher

By Vic Pollard

Reprinted from *California Journal*, June 1994

The veteran legislative staffer's voice shook with nervousness, and he repeatedly declined to answer questions without a guarantee of anonymity. What made the interview unusual was that he wasn't being asked about his boss' politics or legislation, subjects on which aides have always been reluctant to be quoted by name. He was being asked about his own career prospects and those of hundreds of other staffers as the Legislature prepares to enter the era of term limits, with the inevitable staff turmoil that will accompany a rapid turnover of lawmakers.

Well, the staffer was asked, how about simply describing the morale among those who toil in offices where most of the employers will be in another line of work, or out of work, in little more than two years?

"I really don't want to be quoted on that," he said emphatically. "Who knows how that could be interpreted by someone?" You never know, he added, who might be reading your resume a year or two from now.

That kind of bunker mentality is common in the Capitol these days as staffers — policy wonks, political hacks and secretaries alike — contemplate their uncertain futures.

"They're all lookin' for jobs," Assembly Speaker Willie Brown Jr. said sadly.

Just three years ago, the staff was stunned by massive layoffs forced by budget cuts under Proposition 140, the term-limits initiative approved by voters in 1990. Some 650 of the Legislature's 2500 staffers accepted "golden handshakes" and moved on to new lives.

Now, the survivors are waiting for the initiative's other shoe to drop: Its limits of three terms in the Assembly and two in the Senate will start forcing large numbers of lawmakers out of office at the end of 1996. By the end of 1998, no one will be left in office who was elected before the initiative passed.

Since nearly everyone who works in the Capitol is hired by a legislator for a personal or committee staff, that portends an unprecedented game of musical chairs among both professional and clerical staffers. And since newly elected lawmakers tend to hire at least some of their aides from their campaign staffs or other sources, the turnover — now about 15 percent a year according to an administrative officer — is expected to accelerate significantly. The difference this time around, however, is that the "golden handshakes" are gone.

The growing instability in the staff worries good-government types like Ruth Holton of Common Cause. "The term-limit proponents kept talking about getting rid of the political hacks," she said. "Well, the political hacks are going to be the last ones to go. It's those with expertise in policy areas who are going to go first."

But the main term-limit proponent — former Los Angeles County Supervisor Pete Schabarum — blames the Legislature itself for Holton's concerns.

"The way the Legislature handled the reduction in dollars available has been outrageous and irresponsible in terms of meeting staffing needs," said Schabarum, who hinted that the argument about loss of institutional memory associated with the departure of long time staff is phony. "The golden handshake was a joke. To offer anybody who wanted to leave a good-bye kiss in terms of substantial dollars is not any way to do it. They needed to select the people who were important to maintaining the integrity of the Legislature and get rid of the political hacks."

No one knows for sure what will happen to the Legislature — and its staff — when term limits are fully implemented and both houses are filled with members who are inexperienced by today's standards. But most observers agree that power, to some extent, will shift away from lawmakers to the people they must depend on for information.

"There will be an enormous shift of power to the staff because they're the only ones with the information, and information is power," says former Republican Senator William Campbell, who now heads the California Manufacturers Association. Many senior staffers say they hope that's what will happen, but they fear it won't. With staffers shifting positions more often and their average years of experience dropping, many worry that institutional memory and skill in crafting legislation will increasingly be the provinces of veteran lobbyists and the governor's office.

"When you're drafting a bill or analyzing a bill, you've got to know all the code sections involved so that you don't have conflicts," said another senior staffer who also declined to be identified. "And you've got to know the history of the issue, so you'll know what worked and what didn't work in the past."

While that's knowledge that can be picked up by time-consuming research, the staffer said that other legislative skills can only be learned in the school of hard knocks. For example, "You've got to know when to look out for the third amendment," he said. "Lobbyists will sometimes put in a bill that looks totally innocent, but what they really want to do won't show up until the third amendment."

Since the bloodletting of 1991, there has been a growing trickle of senior staffers to lobbying and public relations firms and other government jobs. "A lot of people over there are looking right now," said Mike Burns, who recently left Democratic Senator Charles Calderon's staff for a better-paying job with the Burson-Marsteller public-relations firm. "They've said to me and some of my colleagues [who also departed], 'Boy, you guys are lucky to get out now.'"

One rush occurred after the 1992 elections. An even bigger one may occur after this year's elections, in which no fewer than 10 members of the Assembly and five senators are running for non-legislative offices, spurred by the pressure of term limits. Total turnover with retirements and election defeats could be twice those numbers in each house.

The first group of staffers to feel the impact of term limits directly will be those who work for former Senate President pro Tempore David Roberti, who must leave the Legislature at the end of this year. Their experience will be watched closely by everyone in the Capitol Annex. Much of Roberti's large pro tem staff was absorbed by his successor, Bill Lockyer, or found jobs elsewhere. Currently working on his personal staff are 10 professional and clerical people, and the Judiciary Committee he chairs employs nine people, said Roberti's chief of staff, Maeley Tom. She will shortly become west coast vice president of Cassidy & Associates — a Washington-based public-affairs firm.

The future of some of the others depends on whether Roberti wins his race for state treasurer, and takes them with him. But others will have to find work with another lawmaker or outside the Capitol. Since most of them are Democrats, they are also anxiously watching the gubernatorial race, noted one staffer. A defeat for GOP incumbent Pete Wilson would open a whole new job market for Democratic staffers, who hold most of the top committee jobs in both houses — not to mention term-limited Democratic lawmakers.

And even if Roberti loses, Lockyer says he has assured the Roberti staffers that he will try to place them in other offices next year. "There will be no Saturday night massacre," he said. That may be a favor Lockyer can do for his predecessor as pro tem, but it's not a promise he can make to large numbers of other staffers who will find themselves without bosses.

Even before the 1991 budget cuts, job insecurity has been an increasing fact of life for legislative staffers in recent years. In the 1960s and '70s, the legislative staff developed originally by former Assembly Speaker Jesse Unruh was a highly regarded professional corps of policy experts.

"There was a very strong sense of professionalism back in those days," said Carl Brakensiek, who was hired by one of Unruh's successors, Bob Moretti, and is now a lobbyist. As late as 1980, then-Speaker Leo McCarthy would not allow new committee chairs to replace their committees' chief consultants.

But that stability began to break down with the more partisan legislative atmosphere of the 1980s. It is becoming increasingly common for new chairs to insist on their own committee staffs and for new legislators to put campaign workers on the legislative payroll. "This is not the place to work if you're looking for job security," said one consultant.

While old-timers may lament the passing of the good old times, it may be a non-issue with the next generation of legislative staffers. Twenty-three-year-old Margot Schmidt, who joined the office staff of Republican Assemblyman Dean Andal of Stockton two years ago and plans to leave later this year for graduate school, may be typical. She doesn't resent the fact that she had to make a fast, steep trip up the learning curve.

"I would assume that institutional memory is important," Schmidt said. "But a lot of that will be available to the new people. They can do the research. It might take them a little longer, but they can do it."

Tom, a veteran of more than 20 years as a legislative staffer, said Schmidt's outlook is becoming more common.

"The Legislature is no longer considered a long-term career occupation [for staffers]," she said. "It's more of a stepping-stone to other opportunities, much like the legislators themselves see it."

TRANSITIONAL PRO TEM?

Bill Lockyer leads the Senate into the era of term limits

by Steve Scott

Reprinted from *California Journal*, November 1994

Earlier this year, as the state budget debate was approaching its end game, Bill Lockyer (D-Hayward) found himself in a familiar position: He was surrounded by reporters after a floor session. The rookie pro tem had just spent a fair bit of energy and time tamping down a fire that had erupted in the tension of the budget denouement. The battle was not the budget itself. Rather, it was an ugly public spat between Senators Dan McCorquodale (D-Modesto) and Steve Peace (D-Chula Vista). At one point, Peace, the Senate's loosest cannon, yelled across the floor that McCorquodale was "a nut case." When a reporter asked about the flap, Lockyer responded with a roll of the eyes that recalled similar expressions of exasperation one might have seen from his predecessor, David Roberti.

"When tensions arise in the Capitol," Lockyer shrugged, "these little blisters tend to arise."

There was a time in California political history when having both Peace and Lockyer in the same house would have been viewed as a sign of the coming Apocalypse. For much of his early career, Bill Lockyer didn't soothe blisters, he caused them. But times have changed, so much so that the 53-year-old Hayward Democrat has become only the third person in two decades to hold the post of president pro tempore of the Senate.

Lockyer's ascension comes at a time of great upheaval in the Legislature, and he faces challenges unimaginable to any of his predecessors. Term limits are likely to accelerate the arrival of bomb-throwers like Peace from the Assembly, where fiery partisanship is practically in the job description. Pressure will be on Lockyer to maintain the customary deliberativeness of the Senate while at the same time mollifying the more partisan members of his own caucus. Lockyer must also manage the surge of power and influence that most believe will flow into the Senate as a result of term limits, since the upper house will likely become the repository of the Legislature's institutional memory. On top of all that, Lockyer must also keep a check on his own partisan impulses, while at the same time following through on the one clear charge he's been given by his caucus: Keep the Democrats in power.

"David Roberti had a luxury Bill Lockyer will never have," observes Assembly Republican Leader Jim Brulte (R-Rancho Cucamonga). "Roberti had significant majorities to work with. Locker's strength or weaknesses will not be relational to his own abilities. It will relate to the solidification of his majority."

To the extent that Brulte is wrong, and ability is a factor,

the new pro tem certainly has the qualifications for leadership. For Lockyer, politics and the California Legislature has been, and remains, his life's work. Born in East Oakland in 1941, Lockyer grew up in the area he now represents, attending San Leandro High School. He earned a political science degree from UC-Berkeley, but his political activism was born not in the classroom, although as a participant in the Berkeley "Free Speech Movement" of the 1960s.

Already an activist in local Democratic circles, Lockyer worked for seven years as an aide to Assemblyman Robert Crown, and when Crown died in 1973, won the special election to replace him, using what were, at the time, unusual techniques. "At that time, a massive lawn-sign campaign, and campaigning to the reduced universe of likely voters were revolutionary ideas," he recalls. Lockyer quickly established himself as a young man in a hurry, but when the speakership beckoned ambitious lawmakers in 1979, Lockyer was content to wait his turn.

"From my observation of the speakership, it seems that half of the time is taken up handling the egos of the place," he said at the time. "Up to now, I've been one of the ones that's needed a temper calmed."

When he moved over to the Senate in 1982, Lockyer found himself serving on, and eventually chairing, the

Lockyer taking oath of office

the "First Amendment scumbags" in the media, and a 1990 scuffle with a trial lawyer lobbyist whom he said threw "a girlie punch" at him. While still in the Assembly, Lockyer was threatened with arrest by Senator Alfred Alquist (D-San Jose) when he refused to leave a hearing room after Alquist had snubbed one of his bills.

Although he concedes this reputation is "part of my baggage," Lockyer insists such behavior is in the past, and that his detractors have to go back several years to find truly erratic behavior. "I think he has worked hard to get [his temper] under control," said Senator Robert Presley (D-Riverside). "It's a moot concern if you get it under control."

A "kinder and gentler" Lockyer was well positioned to step into leadership, and when the term-limited Roberti let it be known that he was going to run for statewide office, Lockyer immediately began lining up the votes to become pro tem. By getting out ahead of the curve, Lockyer insists he was able to get the votes he needed without making cutting individual deals for chairmanships or staff. Still, his mere acceptance of the job implied one huge promise to his Democratic colleagues: Don't lose control of the Senate.

powerful Judiciary Committee, even though he was still attending law school at night. When he took his bar exam, there was, he recalls, "considerable press interest: 'Will the chair of Judiciary pass the bar?'" He did, and established himself as a master at the insider game. Lockyer was one of those who negotiated the infamous "napkin deal" altering the state's liability laws, which was worked out among lawmakers and lobbyists at Frank Fat's restaurant two days before the end of the 1987 session. Lockyer, in fact, displayed the napkin on the floor of the Senate the night the bill was passed.

Lockyer with Ken Maddy

After he took over for Roberti in late January, Lockyer moved to assuage early concerns that his leadership would be more partisan than Roberti's. Senate Minority Leader Ken Maddy (R-Fresno), who had been one of the early skeptics about Lockyer's ability to tone down the partisanship, says he was satisfied with Lockyer's even-handedness in his first session. "He has tried very hard to accommodate everyone in the Senate, particularly the minority party," concedes Maddy. "He has attempted to keep most things status quo." Lockyer's handling of his first budget negotiations earned him points for being tough, but practical, and his more mercurial tendencies remained firmly in remission.

While working his way up the legislative ladder, Lockyer's policy reputation was of someone who liked to push big ideas. In the Assembly, Lockyer introduced the first legislation to promote the concept of "comparable worth" for traditionally female occupations. Four years before it became a political litmus test, Lockyer introduced the first three-strikes-you're-out law for serious felonies. He wrote the first "Lemon Law" protecting automobile purchasers, and was an early advocate of legislation to keep large companies from filing harassing lawsuits against citizens. Lockyer's policy direction is informed by what he calls his "philosophical and temperamental sympathy for the rebellion in life," but he hastens to add that he does not share what he considers the more naive aspects of classical liberalism. "I'm much more sensitive to matters of history, tradition, and community."

Still, this rebellious spirit may have played a role in the development of Lockyer's more widely-known reputation — the one for temperamental instability. Stories of Lockyer's emotional outbursts are the stuff of Capitol legend. Tales include criticizing Senator Diane Watson (D-Los Angeles) during a committee hearing for "mindless blather," a pass he made at a UPI reporter which was followed by an attack on

"He has been in total control of himself since the word go," says Senator Leroy Greene (D-Sacramento). "It was a relief to some of us who thought 'well, he's OK now, but what happens if he blows?' He didn't blow."

Keeping the Senate's traditional decorum intact didn't mean, however, that Lockyer had turned the house over to the GOP. As Roberti had during his first session as pro tem, Lockyer used the Senate's confirmation authority as a tool to establish his political *bona fides*. Two of Governor Pete Wilson's appointments — one to the UC Regents, the other to the CSU Board of Trustees — were shot down by Lockyer through his position as the chairman of the Senate Rules Committee. It was the first time in 111 years that a UC Regent appointment had been rejected by the Senate. While he kept the Senate from dissolving into a circus during the budget, Lockyer did engineer a show vote on an extension of a 1991 tax hike on the wealthy, and he says he was the only one of the "Big Five" who didn't want to "just get through the year."

Although he didn't make any wholesale changes, Lockyer is taking steps to put his own stamp on the administration of the house. His most controversial administrative step to date has been his decision to appoint the next session's committee chairs on the last day of this year's session. Lockyer moved some existing chairs into new roles, and elevated a number of less-tenured members into prominence. He also proposed creation of a separate Criminal Procedure Committee, comparable to the Assembly's Public Safety Committee, to take some of Judiciary's crime load.

Republicans charged that the committee assignments, and the decision to announce them early, point the way toward more partisanship from Lockyer in the future. "A lot of us were taken aback by it," says Senator Bill Leonard (R-Redlands). "He seemed like he was trying to solidify his leadership by keeping all parties in his caucus as happy as can be." Leonard says the appointment of Senator Tom Hayden (D-Santa Monica), an ardent environmentalist, to chair Natural Resources puts the Democrats "squarely at the far left end of the discussion" on environmental issues. For his part, Lockyer insists the move was simply aimed at insuring a smooth transition by giving prospective chairs a head start on organizing for the new session.

"The debate for me was simply one of whether to wait for January," says Lockyer. "Theoretically, you'd enhance your position [politically] by keeping everyone guessing."

Whatever Lockyer may have done for the organization and policy direction of the Senate so far, his biggest challenge as pro tem began in earnest when the session ended last month. Fourteen of the 20 seats up for grabs in the November election began the campaign in Democratic hands. Several have been, to varying degrees, contested. With the Democrats sitting at 22 by session's end, a loss of two seats could force him to cut deals with independents Quentin Kopp and Lucy Killea in order to retain power next year. "He's been handed a challenge that is almost overwhelming, with the number of races, the number of campaigns, the Republican surge, and the decline in voting by the Democratic base," says Hayden.

Lockyer began tackling that particular challenge even before he officially took over as pro tem. Throughout the 1993 interim, Lockyer worked six days a week on fund raising. When making his pitch in person, Lockyer brought along a stack of charts, *a la* Ross Perot, laying out the case for his party's continued control of the Senate. His chief target in these presentations was what he calls the "theocratic right," as personified by conservative GOP Senator Rob Hurtt (R-Garden Grove) and his Allied Business PAC. Lockyer has also made it his business to reverse what he sees as a tendency for contributors to favor the more flamboyant and well-connected Willie Brown's Assembly leadership caucus. "They develop some history with Willie, so it's almost autopilot," he says. "If they are going to contribute to Democratic races ... the Senate is entitled to equal treatment."

Even with all this effort, Lockyer faced an uphill climb to keep his numbers steady. Republicans say the narrow margin makes Lockyer's leadership tenuous at best. Any further narrowing of the margin would, according to Maddy "suggest all kinds of things for potential coalitions. There's a group of Democrats that don't like Lockyer." Democrats insist Lockyer won't be weakened, even in the wake of possible election setbacks. "As long as Democrats and the independents control, he's fine," says Hayden.

"Serving as leader when so many Democrats are exposed is a particularly thankless job," adds Senator Pat Johnston (D-Stockton). "It's not credible to suggest that [Lockyer] was anything less than totally committed and quite successful in supporting our candidates."

Assuming Lockyer's still exercising functional power come next year, he faces an even more uncertain task: guiding the Senate into the term-limit era. "The power of the pro tem is probably going to be enhanced somewhat, and the power of the speaker will be reduced," offered professor Larry Berg, who directs USC's Unruh Institute on Politics. Berg's suggestion echoes an assessment shared by most in the Legislature, many of whom suggest the only thing keeping the Senate from rolling over the Assembly now is the experience and savvy of Willie Brown.

"The Senate will probably be the center of political stability and innovation in California," Lockyer says. "I have to, in collaboration with my colleagues, create a new, more dynamic Senate." That, in Lockyer's view, means taking steps to modernize the Senate technologically, keeping hold of the Senate's more experienced staffers, and doing a better job of controlling the flow of legislation. An early indication of how he will do might have come the last night of session: The Senate adjourned an unheard-of four hours *before* the midnight deadline rather than the more-typical four hours after.

Lockyer's Democratic colleagues see him as an excellent person to handle the transition to the new order. "He's indefatigable," says Hayden. "Those who've watched him for awhile know that he likes doing this. He'll go the extra mile." Greene says Lockyer's experience in both houses and as a player in policy issues give him the experience base to insure maintenance of an institutional memory. Johnston says Lockyer brings not only a good balance of policy and political skills, but also what he described as a "refreshing candor and directness" to the job.

Republicans offer a less flattering vision of the future. "The one thing that's more possible with Lockyer than with Roberti is an all-out war situation," says Maddy. "He's always volatile. You never know when he's going to blow up." Leonard says that, as long as the margin remains narrow, he sees coalitions in which the GOP teams with different sets of Democrats on different issues. "His [Lockyer's] will wind up being more of an administrative leadership," says Leonard.

Outside observers say it's still too early to predict how a Lockyer leadership will ultimately pan out, because the full impact of term limits likely won't be felt until 1996, when Willie Brown leaves the Assembly. Berg suggests Lockyer's ability to balance the conflicting impulses of stability and partisanship will say much about how the Senate moves into its new era.

"In leadership politics, the personality and skills of the individual may will be the critical factor," says Berg. "Bill Lockyer has a basic idea where he wants the institution to go. That is extremely important." If his words are any indication, Lockyer understands his role in shaping the future of the Legislative branch.

"I'm a transitional pro tem between the old Senate and what will eventually emerge as the new Senate," he says. "I think I have the appropriate combination of political and policy skills for that time." 🏛

LOBBYING & INTEREST GROUPS

The Political Reform Act of 1974 helped reshape relations between lobbyists and legislators. Prior to enactment of this proposition, legislative advocates spent a great deal of time and money entertaining lawmakers and thus winning their favor (and their votes). But the 1974 act prohibited a legislator from taking more than $10 a month from a lobbyist, barred lobbyists from "arranging" for campaign contributions from their clients (this provision has since been invalidated by the courts), established extensive and detailed expense and income reporting requirements, and established the Fair Political Practices Commission to implement the law. The measure has been reasonably successful in cutting the entertainment tie between legislators and advocates and began modifying the way of life in the Capitol. Actually, the system had started to change in 1966 when the Legislature became a full-time body. Many lawmakers and lobbyists brought their families to Sacramento, reducing time available for socializing. In addition under the terms of the ethics measure, Proposition 112 of June 1990 members are: 1) barred from accepting honoraria (payments for speeches), 2) prohibited from receiving compensation for appearing before a state board or agency, 3) limited in the acceptance of gifts from special interests, 4) prohibited from accepting any compensation from lobbyists, 5) required to wait one year after leaving legislative sevrvice before filing as a lobbyist, 6) required to attend ethics training at the begining of each legislative session. In addition, the measure established the California Citizens Compensation Commission to set salaries for elected officals.

The system today is a far cry from the 1930's and 40's when the late Artie Samish boasted: "To hell with the Governor of California! I'm the Governor of the Legislature." And the state's archetypical lobbyist then was probably right. In his long reign, hardly a bill passed the Legislature without Samish's approval. He raised about $1 million over a six-year period from a nickel-a-barrel levy on beer provided by his biggest client and spent it getting legislators "elected and unelected," as he liked to put it. Until 1953 when he was convicted for income-tax evasion, Samish dominated Sacramento; other lobbyists were virtually powerless by comparison. Samish's downfall began when he was interviewed for Collier's magazine and posed with a ventriloquist's dummy he called "Mr. Legislature." The resulting embarrassment prodded the Legislature to pass a mild "reform act" regulating "legislative advocates" in Sacramento. But if the activities of lobbyists are not as blatant as in Samish's day, their power continues unabated. Indeed, the increasing costs of running for election — campaigning for a hotly contested Assembly seat can cost more than $1 million — has made lobbyists and the firms that employ them more important than ever. Moreover, the Legislature in recent years has been plagued with a new round of scandals set off by a "sting" operation run by the FBI and the U.S. Attorney's office. Four Senators were convicted for taking money to help secure passage of the FBI's phony legislative proposal, a bill that would have subsidized a shrimp-packing plant on the Sacramento River.

One Assembly member, a major lobbyist and several staff members were also convicted or pled guilty by mid-1994.

Types of lobbyists

The corps of advocates includes almost every interest group in the state. In 1995 some 1000 advocates are registered. They fall into several categories:

• *Contract lobbyists.* These advocates will work for almost any client willing to pay their fee. The most successful of them charge high prices, make substantial campaign contributions and get results.

• *Corporation and trade association lobbyists.* These advocates work for one company and represent only the interests of their firms, although they often work in tandem with other lobbyists trying to reach the same goal.

• *Public agency lobbyists.* Aside from the associations representing public agencies, numerous cities, counties and special districts maintain their own representatives in Sacramento. And most state agencies have "legislative liaisons," though they are not required to register.

• *"Brown-bag" lobbyists.* These advocates represent interests seeking reforms in a variety of so-called public-interest fields. They include numerous organizations with budgets sufficient only for bag lunches.

Lobbying process

Lobbyists operate in several ways. They provide information and arguments on pending legislation in an attempt to win legislators to their point of view. This information function is a legitimate part of the Legislature's work as it helps define issues. Lobbyists also: have their memberships apply pressure; establish friendships with legislators and wine and dine them; and contribute sometimes substantial amounts to campaigns. Lobbyists also lobby the governor, the bureaucracy, regulatory commissions, the courts and the public.

Lobbyists succeed because there are a great many bills considered each year about which lawmakers have relatively little knowledge or interest, and a word from a lobbyist may tip the balance. A smart lobbyist knows he or she is wasting time trying to persuade a legislator who has a firm philosophical commitment to one side or another on an issue, and so focuses on the uncommitted lawmaker. All legislators are susceptible to persuasion by representatives of interest groups. But some are more attuned, for example, to corporate spokesmen, while others are more apt to go along with a representative of an environmental organization.

In the term limits era at the capitol it will be much harder for lobbyists to develop friendships with the turnstile-members. More of the lobby focus will likely shift to grassroots lobbying: letter writing or fax campaigns, plugging local members into candidates' campaign staffs, and bringing the membership to the capitol for meetings with elected officials and/or rallies and demonstrations. However, rookie legislators may need to look to veteran, savvy lobbyists for help. After all, there are no term limits for lobbyists. 🏛

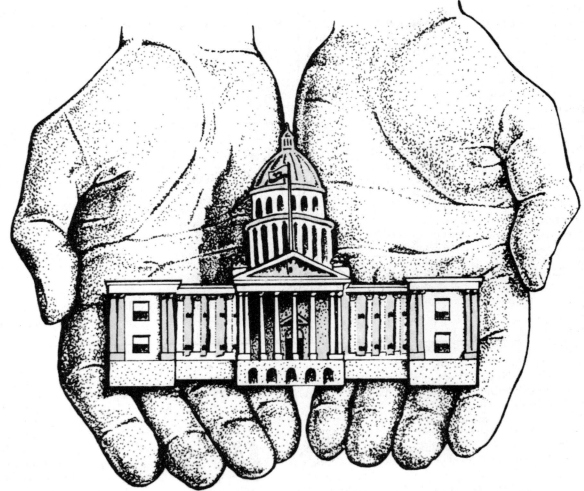

illustration by Patricia Lyn Tweten

Advocacy in the age of term limits

Lobbying after Proposition 140

Reprinted from *California Journal*, October 1993

By Charles Price

I t never takes much to get a politician talking during an election year, and it seemed the one doing the most talking during 1990 election wasn't even running for office. Pete Schabarum, then a Los Angeles County supervisor, was on the hustings a lot during 1990, hawking Proposition 140, the term limit and legislative budget-cutting initiative. Schabarum would start spinning his term-limit spiel at the drop of the hat, and invariably

Charles Price is a professor of government at California State University, Chico, and a frequent contributor to California Journal.

the topic would turn to "special interests."

"Proposition 140 will remove the grip that vested interests have over the Legislature," thundered Schabarum, to anyone who would listen. "It will put an end to the life-time legislators, who have developed cozy relationships with special interests." Term-limited legislators, it was argued, would be more attuned to the public than they would be to "lobbyists and power brokers" generically identified with most of the evils of politics and government.

Well, the public bit hard on Schabarum's bait, approving both Proposition 140 and the follow-up Proposition 164 in 1992, which limited the terms of California's members of

CAREER LOBBYISTS
(6 or more years of experience)

Classification	Number	%
multiple contract firms	232	55
corporation	31	7
trade association	31	7
local government	29	6
public interest	26	6
professions/employees	26	6
labor	14	3
farm	11	3
utilities	9	2
health	7	2
miscellaneous	8	2
TOTAL	**424**	**100**

LOBBYING TOTALS: 1975-1995

Year	#Lobbyists	#Employers	$Spent
'75-76	630	795	40,018,666
'77-78	582	760	49,656,908
'79-80	613	857	59,023,150
'81-82	638	1041	58,345,176
'83-84	753	1338	112,519,158
'85-86	838	1695	137,594,247
'87-88	825	1544	158,498,208
'89-90	817	1537	193,578,059
'91-92	886	1455	116,465,129
'93-94	1021	1568	--
'95-96	1057	1723	

Congress. But while most of the focus of the term-limit debate has centered on its effect on career politicians, those "power brokers" continue to quietly ply their trade. Many believe their influence — particularly that of veteran, "career" lobbyists — will increase geometrically when term-limits fully hit their stride in 1996.

Lobbyists have always had a substantial influence in the affairs of California government and politics. Tall tales about the legendary Artie Samish keeping governors cooling their heels in his office abound from those around during the so-called "Golden Days." However, ever since the rules on lobbying tightened following the passage of the 1974 Political Reform Act, lobbyists continued to play a dramatic role in Capitol politics. One reason is sheer numbers.

There are 1021 registered lobbyists in Sacramento — about nine lobbyists for every legislator and more than a third again as many as were around at the time the Reform Act was approved by voters. Just about every group with a product to peddle or an axe to grind has someone on the payroll or on retainer in Sacramento to lobby their interests with the Legislature and the administration. Roughly 41 percent of these lobbyists are what could be classified career lobbyists — six or more years of experience. Veteran lobbyists tend to be white, male and middle-aged — few are African-American or Latino, only about 20 percent are women.

The lobbyists that enjoy the greatest success tend to be those who have been around awhile. "A lobbyist's experience is an important dimension in lobbying," notes Dugald Gillies, a lobbyist in Sacramento since 1967. "Lobbyists who have a public policy memory can be invaluable."

Lobbyists often develop close personal relationships with legislators, relationships that help them gain access and trust. "There are no great lobbyists," veteran lobbyist Judge James D. Garibaldi said shortly before his recent death. "There are only lobbyists with great friends across the street [at the Capitol]."

Until now, the experience of lobbyists has been offset more or less by the experience of legislators themselves. Roughly 11 percent of the lobbyists currently working in Sacramento have 18 or more years' experience in advocacy. By contrast, 16 percent of legislators — 19 out of 120 — have been around that long. Until his death, Garibaldi was the dean of the Third House, having started his lobbying career in 1946. But that still put him behind the dean of the Legislature — Democratic Senator Ralph Dills of Los Angeles, who began his Assembly career in 1938.

As Proposition 140's limits begin to take effect, however, this dynamic will change. Assembly members will be limited to six years in office, with senators limited to a maximum of eight years. This means that the longest any legislator will be able to serve is 14 years — less time than that 11 percent of lobbyists that have been around since 1975. Currently, 41 percent of all lobbyists have been around for at least six years (see chart above). By 1997, if current trends continue, as much as half the lobbying corps will have spent more time in Sacramento than *any* member of the state Assembly — a situation that could be exacerbated when all of those term-limited ex-lawmakers begin lobbying after sitting on the sidelines for the one year mandated by law.

In this kind of environment, the veteran advocate, and his or her client, has a clear advantage. "It takes a couple of terms to learn something about the process," said Garibaldi.

"I've got a store of knowledge on wholesale liquor issues that goes back 37 years." Patricia Hewitt, who became one of the first women to work as a contract lobbyist in 1971, agrees. "Experience is critical to lobbying," says Hewitt. "After you get known as knowledgeable in a policy area, legislators and staff will call to get your input on pending legislation."

Since experience is a valuable commodity in any profession, the most veteran lobbyists tend to represent major economic interests and large mass membership groups — the entities with the wherewithal to afford the best. Much of this activity centers around large, multiple-contract lobbying firms — more than half the career lobbyists either run or work for multiple contract firms (see chart, page 30). Most of these firms have one or two lobbyists, representing five to 10 clients. But some of the Capitol's "Jurassic Park" of lobbying have grown to Rexian size. George Steffes employs eight lobbyists and serves 64 clients. Advocation, California Advocates and Sacramento Advocates all employ between three and six lobbyists and carry from 37 to 46 clients. Some of the biggest of the big-shot clients use more than one lobbying firm. Browning-Ferris Industries is represented by no fewer than five lobbying firms. Phillip Morris uses four different firms, and R.J. Reynolds and Whittle Communications each use three firms.

Adding to the strength and continuity of these firms is the people they choose as lobbyists. Some, like Garibaldi and former Senators John Foran and Dennis Carpenter, are ex-legislators. Others include former legislative staff, veterans of prior administrations and governmental agencies, and well-connected lawyers. A large number of career lobbyist firms employ spouses, siblings and sons or daughters, thereby heightening continuity. And then there are trade organizations, which can operate like contract lobbying firms in the manner in which they employ lobbyists. The California Farm Bureau employs nine lobbyists, and seven of the nine are careerists — three of them with more than 18 years experience.

What it all boils down to is knowledge, and in a term-limited Legislature, knowledge translates to power. Without veteran legislators around to "remember when," lobbyists will possess the institutional memory, shaded, no doubt, to reflect the interests of their clients. Moreover, budget cuts imposed by Proposition 140 will mean that legislators will have fewer policy staff experts on the payroll. Lobbyists could wind up becoming surrogate staffers, allowing savvy advocates to not only re-invent the past, but shape the present to their clients' advantage.

"In 1961, the Federal Arsenal at Benicia was slated to be closed," recalls lobbyist Gillies. "I helped put together legislation to allow the city to acquire this property. Now, several legislators have talked to me about using this same principle in their communities with various base closings. Nobody else around here knew about the previous legislation. That's knowledge."

Despite a general sense that experience will help lobbyists gain an edge under term limits, some warn that the experience advantage may be offset by some distinct institutional disadvantages. These disadvantages, argue some, may actually make it tougher for lobbyists familiar with the glad-handing and back-slapping of the "good old days."

For one thing, many of the new arrivals view themselves as "reformers", and thus, tend to be suspicious of lobbyists.

"Some of these new legislators won't even talk to you," sniffed an exasperated Garibaldi when asked about the 1992 crop. "[They] have a perception that lobbyists are terrible people," adds Hewitt.

Another development that complicates the traditional means of lobbying is the decline of social interaction between lobbyists and legislators. "In the old days, we used to have lunches together and lobbyists, senators and Assembly members got to know each other," recalls Grant Kenyon, long-time lobbyist for the California Restaurant Association. "The rule was that lobbyists would never discuss legislation at these gatherings — just socialize."

Many veteran lobbyists warn that this suspicion and distance could backfire on legislators and, ultimately, make the process less efficient and effective. Many view their experience as a tool that will help make the transition to the post-140 world smoother, if it is used.

"In the business world, people work together over long periods of time," says Kenyon. "That won't be the case with term limits."

Of course, one class of lobbyist will always be welcome — those whose clients also give out campaign contributions. While the terms of office may have changed, the campaign finance rules haven't, and fund-raising becomes even more urgent. "Today, the main interaction between legislators and lobbyists is at fund raisers," says 33-year veteran lobbyist Richard Ratcliff. "I understand from a legislator's standpoint that they have only so much time. They have to raise campaign money, so they have to prioritize who they see based on this."

"This session [the first under term limits] has been business as usual," says 26-year pro Mike Dillon. "My guess is that lobbyists that represent groups with PACs will have a distinct advantage in gaining access."

Still, there are some who see term limits as helping those lobbyists who represent trade, labor and public-interest associations. Leslie Howe, who has lobbied since 1959 and currently represents the California Retailers Association, believes there will be more emphasis on grass-roots lobbying because of the increased turnover occasioned by term-limits. "New legislators are likelier to respond to an interest group's local constituents rather than their Capitol lobbyists," says Howe.

And even if newcomers are suspicious of lobbyists at first, most veteran advocates believe the rookies will eventually seek them out, if for no other reason than simple desperation.

"There's a bill that's been introduced that, if I had known the author, wouldn't have seen the light of day," says Kenyon. "How in the world will people acquire enough knowledge in just four years to be chair of the water committee, for example?"

So what about those "cozy relationships" between special interests and legislators. Will they diminish under Proposition 140? Hardly. Expertise and know-how will continue to reside in the Third House, as will the ever-present pipeline to campaign money. Term-limits mean more turnover, more open seats, and more influence for the lobbyists whose clients can pour money into those seats. And when a lawmaker's time is up, lobbyists can point the way to post-Legislature employment — another of the potential dangers most feared by term-limit opponents. In any case, what the future promises in the Legislature is weak leaders, instability and rapid turnover. What the future holds in the lobbying community is seniority, expertise and influence. 🏛

"Astroturf lobbying"

Powerful (and not-always-popular) special interests influence the Legislature from behind the shield of others

By Bill Ainsworth

Reprinted from California Journal, November 1994

When state Senator Leroy Greene's (D-Carmichael) office received a barrage of calls this past April from senior citizens supporting a bill backed by oil companies, his staff wondered why so many Sacramentans were interested in such an obscure issue. But as the calls started tying up his phone lines, a seething Greene realized he was on the receiving end of an elaborate — and he says deceptive — public-relations blitz.

The lobbying campaign is one front in a war that oil companies are waging against California regulations requiring auto companies to sell electric cars. The industry spent hundreds of thousands of dollars to generate phone calls and postcards from ordinary citizens to create the illusion of grass-roots support for the bill.

The bill itself would have made it more difficult for utilities to service electric cars. But instead of broadcasting its own support for the legislation, the oil industry enlisted the help of a respected consumer group, Toward Utility Rate Normalization. TURN, which believed the legislation would prevent utility bills from going up, lent its name to a mass mailing that the oil companies quietly bankrolled. The bill itself quietly died before the end of the legislative session.

The oil industry's effort is just the latest example of an increasingly popular lobbying technique — termed "astroturf" by critics because the "grass-roots" are artificial. Three years ago the insurance industry spent $1.5 million encouraging citizens to write and call legislators to express support for no-fault auto insurance. During the past year, Philip Morris has spent hundreds of thousands of dollars to drum up small-business opposition to smoking restrictions. These efforts allow unpopular special interests to hide behind "white hat" groups — such as consumer activists, environmentalists, senior citizens and small business owners — whose motives are considered above suspicion. In some cases the public-relations firms hired by special interests actually create "grass-roots" groups.

As part of "astroturf" campaigns, the businesses fund phone banks, petition drives and mass mailings — methods refined by citizens' groups.

"Big business tries to make it look like they have a bunch of citizen support," says Ruth Holton, executive director of California Common Cause. "It's extremely deceptive." Such campaigns, Holton says, undermine efforts by genuine citizen activists. "How is a legislator going to tell the difference between a big business effort and a genuine effort?"

Assemblyman Terry Friedman (D-Los Angeles) first encountered "astroturf" campaigns while sponsoring anti-smoking legislation. His AB 13 banned smoking in all indoor restaurants and nearly all workplaces. Tobacco industry lobbyists decided that a lobbying campaign led by tobacco barons might not impress lawmakers. Instead, they decided to find ordinary, salt-of-the-earth citizens who also opposed the restrictions. The industry's high-powered, high-priced public-relations firm organized "grass-roots" small business owners and ferried some of them to Sacramento.

Meanwhile, Philip Morris already had experience creating and sustaining "grass-roots" groups. Three years ago, the tobacco giant hired the Dolphin Group, a Los Angeles public-relations firm, to form the California Business and Restaurant Alliance. Friedman calls it a front group for the tobacco industry. Located in the Dolphin Group offices, the alliance has recruited witnesses, published newsletters, and commissioned economic studies against local smoking restrictions.

Last year, when Friedman threatened statewide restrictions, the alliance turned its attention to Sacramento. Alliance members testified eloquently against AB 13 at a Senate Judiciary Committee hearing in April. Their opposition was especially helpful because the established restaurant group, the California Restaurant Association, supported the bill. One witness, Maurice Prince, told the committee that the anti-smoking bill would drive customers away from her popular Los Angeles eatery, Maurice's Snack & Chat. "I hate for you to tell me what I can do with my restaurant," she said. "I have worked day and night for my restaurant." Prince, who was later whisked from the hearing by a tobacco industry driver, said she was recruited into the effort by the Dolphin Group.

Tobacco lobbyists had shrewdly arranged for witnesses from key senators' districts. Prince, for example, owns a restaurant in Senator Diane Watson's (D-Los Angeles) district, while Rudy Martinez, another witness, owns a restaurant in Senator Art Torres' (D-Los Angeles) district. Both lawmakers are sensitive to problems faced by minority business owners.

After the testimony, Torres and another Los Angeles-area Democrat, Charles Calderon, moved to gut AB 13 by allowing smoking in restaurants

---

Bill Ainsworth is a Sacramento reporter for the San Francisco Recorder.

and wiping out tough local ordinances. Both senators said they were responding to the testimony by "grass-roots" opponents. "I'm concerned about [Martinez'] restaurant because that's in my district," said Torres at the hearing.

Torres later changed his mind and dropped his amendments after Friedman threw a fit. A candidate for insurance commissioner, he had been stung by criticism that he was hiding behind "grass-roots" opposition while actually doing the bidding of the tobacco industry.

Dolphin Group President Lee Stitzenberger, however, denied that his firm was running an "astroturf" campaign. "These aren't people made out of whole cloth. They are concerned business people who oppose smoking restrictions."

Friedman's bill eventually passed the Legislature and was signed into law by Governor Pete Wilson. It would be overturned, however, by the passage this month of Proposition 188, also sponsored in large measure by Philip Morris. The campaign to pass the initiative is being run by The Dolphin Group.

In its campaign against Friedman's anti-smoking bill, the tobacco industry created a new "grass-roots" opposition group. In another recent astroturf campaign, the oil industry exploited its alliance with an existing citizens' group — TURN. Earlier this year, TURN, which fights to keep utility bills low, sponsored legislation to make it more difficult for utilities to invest $600 million in the equipment needed to service electric cars. Under California anti-pollution regulations, by the year 1998, electric cars must make up 2 percent of the sales of major automakers. TURN argues that the investments are so speculative that utility company shareholders, not ratepayers, should bear any risk associated with them. Utilities and their environmentalist allies disagree, contending that the investments will help them manage their electricity more efficiently and eventually lead to lower rates.

Oil companies quickly realized that the bill had important implications for the future of electric cars. Without a large investment in charging facilities, electric cars cannot be driven conveniently. The Western States Petroleum Association, the oil industry trade group, wrote a letter to senators on the energy committee, arguing that the investments amount to an unfair subsidy to a competitor.

But the association's public-relations firm, Burlingame-based Woodward & McDowell, did not bring oil-company executives to Sacramento to testify for the bill in public. Instead, it organized "Californians Against Utility Company Abuses," a coalition including TURN, the California Manufacturers Association and other large energy users. Next, the firm sent 200,000 letters to taxpayers, urging them to stop a plan "cooked up" by utilities to "increase your gas and electric rates by $600 million to subsidize their profit-making ventures."

Warning that "powerful utility company lobbyists are already working behind the scenes to defeat these consumer-protection bills," the letter urged citizens to return postcards supporting TURN's legislation. It was signed by Audrie Krause, executive director of TURN, and Howard Owens, director of the Congress of California Seniors. The citizens who received the letter were not told that it had been written by the oil industry's public-relations firm and paid for by the industry.

Provoked by the alarming letter, 50,000 people returned postcards to Woodward & McDowell, which then forwarded the cards to legislators' offices. The firm then organized phone banks. It called citizens who had returned the postcards, and patched them in directly to the offices of their lawmakers. The phone banks targeted the 11 members of the Senate energy committee, which planned hearings on Senate Bill 1819. In this case, however, the campaign may have been too elaborate for its own good. Many citizens were confused by the calls from the phone bank. When they were patched in to government offices, some did not know whether they opposed or supported the bill.

Senator Greene said his district and Capitol offices took calls for two days from constituents who believed that his office was calling them. His staff members grew increasingly irritated. At the hearing, Greene and other senators were so angry that they forced the bill's author, Senator David Kelly (R-Hemet), to put it on hold.

Senator Steve Peace (D-Chula Vista) called the campaign a "sleazy tactic" because the mailing failed to mention oil-company funding. "You ought to make a public apology to every member of the Legislature," Peace told oil lobbyists.

Senator Tom Hayden (D-Santa Monica) said TURN's alliance with the oil industry had tainted the consumer group. "I find it to be the end of the independence of TURN," he said. Krause insisted that her group's association with the oil industry does not compromise its independence. She and oil industry representative Scott Macdonald of Woodward & McDowell defended their effort, arguing that it was a coalition, not an "astroturf" campaign.

"These are concerned citizens responding to an issue that is important to them," said Macdonald.

Both the tobacco and oil industry campaigns demonstrate the increasing sophistication of statehouse lobbying. It used to be enough for tobacco and oil lobbyists to strut around the Capitol, whispering in lawmakers' ears and making strategic donations. Now, however, these and other industries have found that their chances of success increase if they build coalitions with citizens' groups — even if they have to invent their own group. Critics charge, however, that the special interests are not only building coalitions with grass-roots groups, but using them — and hiding behind them — for their own selfish purposes.

"These guys should have built the Stealth bomber," said one supporter of Friedman's anti-smoking bill. "They are so good at disguising themselves."

Common Cause supported a bill by Terry Friedman this year that would have required more complete financial disclosure of astroturf and other lobbying campaigns. Under its provisions, clients of lobbyists would have had to itemize the money they spend on activities like economic studies, phone banks and public-relations campaigns.

"They shouldn't be able to hide their activities," Friedman said. "This is a sunshine bill."

At the end of the 1993-94 session, the California Manufacturers Association helped defeat Friedman's bill, arguing that it would have imposed burdensome record-keeping requirements. Although Friedman himself is leaving the Legislature to become a Los Angeles judge, Common Cause's Ruth Holton plans to seek a new author next year. She expects to see lobbyists rely more on public-relations experts to mobilize support for their clients' positions because term limits will weaken their relationships with lawmakers. 🏛

PARTIES, POLITICS & ELECTIONS

Political Parties

By both design and tradition, political parties in California are exceptionally weak — especially when compared to the machine politics prevalent in some eastern states. The weakening of the party structure was engineered by Hiram Johnson and the Progressives starting in 1911 as a reaction to the machine politics of the railroad interests and San Francisco boss Abe Ruef. Parties were explicitly forbidden from endorsing in non-partisan contests and implicitly from making pre-primary endorsements in partisan contests for much of this century. All local offices and judgeships were made nonpartisan, and a unique method of running, called cross-filing, was instituted. Numerous provisions were written into the law for the express purpose of reducing party power, and many of these restrictions remain in the law today. An independent spirit was fostered in California, and even now there are parts of the state where the electorate pays very little attention to a candidate's party. It is these areas — notably the San Joaquin Valley and the rural districts that can hold the balance of power in state elections.

Under cross-filing, which lasted from 1914 to 1959, a candidate could file for the nomination of not only his or her own party but other parties as well (and until 1952, without any indication of party affiliation). This had the effect of weakening party structure and making pressure groups and the press more important. It also led to the election of popular candidates in the primary, when they won both the Republican and Democratic nominations. Generally, cross-filing helped Republicans more than Democrats, and it is probably significant that Democrats have done much better in elections since the system was eliminated in favor of traditional primaries.

California now has six official parties — Democratic, Republican, Libertarian, Peace and Freedom, American Independent, and the Green Party. A party can win official status by getting the signatures of one percent of the registered voters or by obtaining a petition signed by a number of voters equal to ten percent of the votes cast for governor in the previous election. To remain official, a party must get two percent of the vote for a statewide candidate and retain one-15th of one percent of registered voters. Loss of official status means that a party can run candidates by write-in only, a difficult assignment in an era of electronic voting.

Party organization

The party structure is spelled out in detail in state law, although some minor variations are allowed for Democrats and Republicans. These are the basic official elements of party structure:

• *National committee members.* These are elected by the delegation to the national convention and serve as the state party's representatives on the national committee of each party.

• *Delegates to national conventions.* Slates are developed by supporters of each primary candidate, and winning delegates — with alterations and additions — cast the state's votes at the quadrennial convention. The winner-take-all primary is used by California Republicans. State Democrats use a proportional representation system of delegates elected from congressional districts. California's primary and presidential primary will be moved ahead on the calendar to the fourth Tuesday in March 1996 to give California voters a greater opportunity to influence presidential nomination politics.

• *County central committees.* These committees, elected directly by the voters, are charged with directing party affairs in each county. In fact, however, these committees are weak, and the real power is held by the office-holders in each county.

• *State central committee.* This committee is comprised of about 1400 members in the GOP and 2500 to 3000 members in the Democratic Party. This committee is charged with electing party officials, managing and operating the party, and selecting presidential electors. An executive committee of the state central committee handles the day-to-day operation of the party.

• *State chairs.* In theory, the chair speaks for the party and develops election strategy in conjunction with the executive committee. With rare exception, however, the main leaders are the major officeholders of both parties.

As noted, Progressive reforms weakened party organization in the state. However, several developments may serve to strengthen California parties in the 1990s:

1) Because of court rulings in the 1980s, parties may now make endorsements in partisan primaries and in nonpartisan contests. Democrats have established detailed regulations for their party on their endorsing rules and format. Republicans have decided, because of potential divisions, not to endorse. Since 1988, (the first year that endorsing went into effect), endorsing has not been a major factor influencing the nomination or election politics of the Democratic Party, but it could evolve into a significant factor in the years ahead because of term limits and many open (no incumbent) districts.

2) Parties have democratized selection to State Central Committees. There are fewer appointments by office-holders, and more elections from the counties. Democrats have created Assembly District Caucuses in the 80 districts to choose 12 delegates per district.

3) Lastly, election by Democrats of Jerry Brown (former governor and ambitious elective office seeker) symbolized the growing importance of the state chair's position. Current state chairs are Bill Press for the Democrats and John Herrington for the Republicans.

POLITICAL PARTY ORGANIZATION

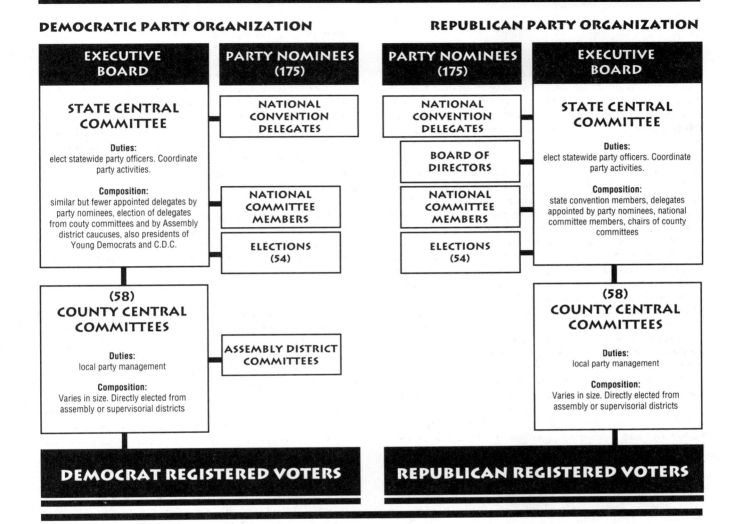

DEMOCRATIC PARTY ORGANIZATION

EXECUTIVE BOARD

STATE CENTRAL COMMITTEE

Duties:
elect statewide party officers. Coordinate party activities.

Composition:
similar but fewer appointed delegates by party nominees, election of delegates from couty committees and by Assembly district caucuses, also presidents of Young Democrats and C.D.C.

PARTY NOMINEES (175)

NATIONAL CONVENTION DELEGATES

NATIONAL COMMITTEE MEMBERS

ELECTIONS (54)

(58) COUNTY CENTRAL COMMITTEES

Duties:
local party management

Composition:
Varies in size. Directly elected from assembly or supervisorial districts

ASSEMBLY DISTRICT COMMITTEES

DEMOCRAT REGISTERED VOTERS

REPUBLICAN PARTY ORGANIZATION

PARTY NOMINEES (175)

NATIONAL CONVENTION DELEGATES

BOARD OF DIRECTORS

NATIONAL COMMITTEE MEMBERS

ELECTIONS (54)

EXECUTIVE BOARD

STATE CENTRAL COMMITTEE

Duties:
elect statewide party officers. Coordinate party activities.

Composition:
state convention members, delegates appointed by party nominees, national committee members, chairs of county committees

(58) COUNTY CENTRAL COMMITTEES

Duties:
local party management

Composition:
Varies in size. Directly elected from assembly or supervisorial districts

REPUBLICAN REGISTERED VOTERS

Elections

A person may register to vote in California who is 18, a citizen of the United States and a resident of the county of registration for at least 30 days prior to the election (and who is otherwise not disqualified, such as in the case of certain felons). There are several types of elections in California:

• *State primaries.* These take place the first Tuesday after the first Monday in June of even-numbered years. At these elections, nominees for national, state and some local offices are selected. Usually, there are a number of propositions also on the ballot.

• *State general elections.* These take place on the first Tuesday after the first Monday in November of even-numbered years, and voters make their selections from among the nominees chosen in the primaries. The ballot usually contains more propositions.

• *Special elections.* These rarely take place on a state-wide basis because of high cost, although there was one in November 1973 when Governor Ronald Reagan put his tax-limitation initiative to a vote (it lost). Special elections are more often held locally to fill vacancies in Congress and the state Legislature. These are different from most other elections in that the voters are given a list of candidates of all parties. If no one candidate receives a simple majority, a runoff is held four weeks later among the top vote-getters in each party. In some cases, this means that candidates far down the list make the runoff while the candidate who finished second in number of votes does not.

• *Local elections.* Often, elections for local city council and special district-director posts are not consolidated with the primary and general elections and are held at various times during the year.

Political History

During the early years of state history, there were rapid political swings based on economics. When things went well, the big-business interests were in control. During a depression period in the 1870s, the Workingmen's Party under Denis Kearney of San Francisco came to power and managed to get much of its program enacted. When prosperity returned, the party disappeared. Economic and political power went into the hands of the "Big Four" — railroad magnates Charles Crocker, Mark Hopkins, Collis P. Huntington and Leland Stanford. Southern Pacific dominated California politics from the 1880s until the advent of the Progressives more than 25 years later.

The Progressives

Republican newspaper editors started in the first decade of this century to drum up opposition to the railroads and the boss of San Francisco, Abe Ruef. Disgruntled Republicans started the Lincoln-Roosevelt league, and graft-fighter Hiram Johnson became the group's candidate for governor. He pledged to kick Southern Pacific out of the Republican Party and out of California government. He won easily and immediately started enacting reforms such as the initiative, referendum, recall, cross-filing, civil service, and a multitude of other programs. Johnson went to the United States Senate in 1916 and was succeeded by another progressive, William D. Stephens. The movement lost its force in the 1920s as postwar prosperity produced political apathy. Until the next depression, the regular Republicans maintained control of state government.

The Great Depression resulted in the 1934 gubernatorial candidacy of muckraking author Upton Sinclair (his slogan: "End Poverty in California") with his radical plan for reforming the economic system. Republican Frank Merriam defeated Sinclair by about a quarter of a million votes. With the Democrats riding high nationally under President Franklin D. Roosevelt, the Republicans finally lost the governorship in 1938 to state Senator Culbert Olson.

Four years later, a new progressive era began under Earl Warren. Aided by cross-filing, the former Alameda County district attorney and state attorney general portrayed himself as a non-partisan official — an image he embroidered later as an activist Chief Justice of the United States. Warren's personal popularity was unprecedented in California political history. He was able to push most of his programs through the Legislature (with a compulsory health-insurance plan the notable exception). Warren was the Republican vice-presidential nominee in 1948 (with Thomas Dewey) and perhaps could have remained governor indefinitely. After 10 years as the state's chief executive, he was named U.S. Chief justice by President Eisenhower in 1953.

The new governor was Goodwin J. Knight, who was reelected in his own right in 1954 but was unable to establish himself as leader of the Republican Party because he had to contend with two other major figures, then-Vice-President Richard Nixon and U.S. Senator William Knowland. In 1958, Knowland decided that for political and personal reasons —

he thought being governor was a better stepping stone to the presidency — he would leave his safe Senate seat to run for governor. Knight was pushed aside and virtually forced to run for Knowland's seat. Knowland embraced a right-to-work initiative, setting the stage for a massive Democratic victory led by the gubernatorial candidate, Edmund G. (Pat) Brown. Nixon, defeated in a 1960 run for president against John F. Kennedy, tried an unsuccessful comeback by running against Brown in 1962.

In his second term, Brown became embroiled in a bitter intra-party fight with the powerful speaker of the Assembly, Jesse M. Unruh, and elected to seek a third term rather than give his arch-rival a clear shot at his job. In the primary election, Brown's forces concentrated on shooting down the moderate Republican candidate, former San Francisco Mayor George Christopher, preferring to run against the conservative Ronald Reagan, a former actor. Somebody goofed: Reagan crushed Brown in the general by a million votes.

Democratic nominee Unruh tried to unseat Reagan four years later. Although plagued by limited financial resources, Unruh cut Reagan's victory margin in half. Reagan kept his 1966 pledge not to seek a third term in 1974, leaving the gates wide open. Twenty-nine candidates ran in the primary, with Brown's son, Jerry, and Houston I. Flournoy emerging from the pack to represent the Democratic and Republican parties in November. Brown won by only 179,000 votes, almost blowing his big early lead. Four years later, he rebounded with a 1.3-million-vote victory over the GOP attorney general, Evelle J. Younger.

In 1982 Jerry Brown continued the two-term limit tradition and ran for U.S. Senator (he lost to San Diego Mayor Pete Wilson, a Republican). Attorney General George Deukmejian won a tough primary against Lieutenant Governor Mike Curb for the Republican party nomination and squeaked past the Democratic candidate, Los Angeles Mayor Tom Bradley, in November.

In a repeat in 1986, Deukmejian trounced Bradley, winning by over a million and a half votes. Alan Cranston won re-election to a fourth term in the U.S. Senate, defeating Republican Rep. Ed Zschau.

Pete Wilson maintained Republican control of the state's chief executive position with his victory over Democrat Dianne Feinstein in November 1990. Wilson's non-ideological, pragmatic philosophy is more in the Warren, not Reagan, mold.

For the first time this century both U.S. Senate seats were up for election in 1992, the extra seat as a result of Pete Wilson's resignation from the Senate, and for the first time in the nation's history two women, Democrats Dianne Feinstein and Barbara Boxer, were elected the the U.S. Senate.

In 1994 Kathleen Brown, Pat's daughter and Jerry's sister, won the Democratic nomination for Governor. She was soundly defeated by Pete Wilson in November after leading by more than 20 points in the polls a year earlier. Feinstein was re-elected to the U.S. Senate after defeating Rep. Michael Huffington by a whisker in the most expensive election in U.S. history.

Consultants at the grass roots

Illustrations by Mike Tofanelli

Professional campaign help goes local

By Clea Benson and John Borland

Reprinted from *California Journal*, November 1994

When you have to go to court, you hire a lawyer. If you have to have your appendix out, you hire a doctor. If your car makes clanking sounds and has smoke coming from the whaddyacallit, you take it to a mechanic.

And to a growing extent, if you are running in a political race in California, even at the most local level, you look for a professional consultant. Increasingly savvy candidates for city council, county supervisor, mayor and even water boards rely on small-time James Carvilles and Mary Matalins to help craft campaign strategies and target likely supporters. It no longer matters who has the best slogan-embossed pot holders and refrigerator magnets. With office-seekers at the grass roots vying for the best high-tech data bases and well-honed lists of targeted voters, consultants have found a new gold mine in the Golden State.

"You can do it yourself, but it's time-consuming and you have to find someone who knows what they're doing," says Harry Moore, a Democrat who hired Marin County consultant Marc O'Hara to run his 1994 campaign for Contra Costa County supervisor. "A campaign manager knows where you should be walking or how thoroughly you should be contacting people."

Clea Benson and John Borland are reporters with California News Service, a project of the Graduate School of Journalism at the University of California, Berkeley.

Consultants who have worked in other parts of the country say the phenomenon is not unique to California. But they agree that this state, long a trend setter for campaign technique, is on the leading edge at the local level.

"In 1937 the first political direct mail went out in Marin County," says Bob Mulholland, campaign adviser for the state Democratic Party. "California's always been at the forefront of campaign technology. Probably in the last 10 years it's really taken off at the local level. It's more true in urban areas just like it's more true in California than in other states."

Precise figures on the number of consultants doing local races are hard to attain. But of the 362 consulting firms listed in the American Association of Political Consultants' directory, 124 are based in California, more than in any other region except Washington, D.C. And observers say the number of consultants in the state has grown rapidly.

"In the 1960s there were only a handful," says Dick Rosengarten, editor of *CalPeek's* state directory of full-time consultants. His latest list, compiled a little more than a year ago, contained 300 entries.

Much of the trend pushing political consultants to the local level is a simple result of the laws of supply and demand. California has precisely the right mix of political resources that make it a natural magnet for consultants: large urban markets, districts from congressional down to city council that are too large and too diverse for a political neophyte to understand, and abundant races, even in off years. Not to mention lots and lots of money.

"California does politics with a vengeance," says Carol Hess, editor of the "Political Resource Directory." "Even in New York — a big state — $100,000 is a lot to spend on a state legislative seat." Not in California, where Assembly seats have been known to go for more than $1 million.

But the number of statewide, congressional and even state Senate and Assembly races is limited, the traditional market for consultants easily saturated. This means the growing ranks of campaign professionals must create demand among lower-level candidates who might otherwise have been happy running with no more help than a group of interested friends. "My pitch is that even

if I charge you a couple of thousand dollars, I can help you save at least that much by targeting your mail," says Los Angeles-area consultant Tom Shortridge, a Republican who started his own firm two years ago after working for former GOP Assemblyman Gerald Felando. "If you're running a full-time consulting firm, you need the business."

At the bread-and-butter level, a full-time consultant needs to fill time, particularly in off-years, with paying clients. This is possible in California only with recourse to local races, special elections and other small-ticket items. "You don't find a lot of people who make enough money to take off the non-election years," says Joe Cerrell, a former president of the AAPC who has worked in California since the late 1950s. But every campaign adviser also seeks reputation and prestige, which for political consultants translates very directly into dollars. "It's the cliche, 'You're as good as your last campaign,'" Cerrell says.

There is a hierarchy among consultants in the state. At the top are those that handle primarily statewide candidates, such as Democrats Clint Reilly and Darry Sragow or Republican Sal Russo. On a slightly lower level are the big names that advise mostly legislative races, with an occasional dip into local politics, such as Democrat Richie Ross or veteran Republicans Ray McNally and Richard Temple. Below them are the mass of consultants who handle local races, usually within a single region. Some, like Reilly, can build their reputation enough to climb up the ranks. But this kind of vertical mobility is unusual.

"It's not really correct to say there is a career ladder that starts at the lower rungs," Sragow says. "It's a very fluid business. But I don't see a lot of movement." To a large extent, local consultants carve out a turf in their own area and concentrate on getting business and winning races there.

Demand is not hard to drum up for consultants with or without big names. Increased competition and new technology have made some kind of professional help affordable even for campaigns with shoestring budgets. Democrat Parke Skelton, who has managed everything from school board races to legislative contests, charges between $5000 and $10,000 to advise a campaign with a $35,000 budget. Shortridge says his fees tend to be about 20 per-

cent of a campaign's total spending. His average local candidate spends about $15,000, he says, though the range has run from as little as $5000 to a $300,000 Los Angeles City Council race.

Consultants, even those without a big following, have more to offer now than in the old days of note cards and file cabinets. Candidates can get computer tapes filled with lists of registered voters and their vital political statistics. A professional with a computer, database, and a little bit of analytical experience can take this raw data and help candidates target their likely supporters with surgical precision. This technology gives candidates more for their consulting dollar. After spawning a new breed of professionals with computer know-how, it has now brought sophistication to local politics and spread power in the consulting industry. "We used to have kingmakers in cities with shoe boxes full of voters," says Shortridge. "These guys are all out of business. Now you can do it all in half a nano-second on a computer."

But local consulting is not just about technology, according to Marc O'Hara, who went back to local campaigns after running Arlo Smith's unsuccessful 1990 bid for state attorney general and Claire Sargent's 1992 race for the U.S. Senate in Arizona. It also means doing traditional things such as walking precincts, albeit in a targeted way. "You can actually create more change in a real and rational way working with local people than you can in multi-million-dollar statewide campaigns because those campaigns don't come in contact with real voters," O'Hara says. "Campaigns on that level do three basic things: raise money, develop messages that are based on research and then deliver those messages in creative ways."

Not every candidate can afford a full package of consulting services. But the demand for sophistication has led to a group of "boutique" firms that give clients a choice of individualized services, such as polling or district surveys, campaign accounting or direct mail. Some of these organizations, previously accustomed to wholesaling their services to full-time consultants, are now working directly with the candidates themselves.

"I have seen more and more local people come to us when they're just shy of being able to hire someone, but they need a little help on the technical end," says Fred Thomas, co-owner of the Chatsworth-based Aaron Group, a company that specializes in direct mail. Thomas' company, which offers a full range of services from design to mailing, has handled jobs as small as $1000 for a small city council race and as large as $100,000 during a hotly contested Los Angeles City Council election.

Sandy Webb, a Libertarian Simi Valley city councilwoman running for re-election, is a good example of a candidate who shops for professional assistance according to her limited budget and pressing needs. During her first campaign four years ago, Webb used a part-time consultant to write campaign material and target supporters and hired a firm to shoot cable television ads. This year, Webb decided not to use a consultant but did contract with the Aaron Group to print and send her direct mail.

"If you have the money in the campaign, I feel it's best to use a service that doesn't just do printing but does the mailing as well," says Webb, who had volunteers stuff her letters in envelopes last time around. "This time I have a little better budget and I just don't need that kind of push [from a consultant]."

Although consultants are based more heavily in urban areas, where prohibitively expensive media markets create a greater demand for targeting services, innovative campaign strategies are filtering out to less-populous regions. "The differences are not as great as you would think," says Sragow, comparing practices in small communities with those in metropolitan areas. Candidates have the same problems in reaching people and eliciting interest across the state. "Voters are as difficult to get to at the local level as for statewide races," he says.

Other features of the California landscape ensure a steady demand for consulting services well into the future. The 1990 legislative reapportionment, drawn by the courts rather than the partisan Legislature, created a larger number of contested districts than usual. And with voters paying less and less attention to traditional methods of campaign advertising, candidates will need consultants to devise new ways to get their messages across.

The passage of Proposition 140, instituting term limits for state constitutional and legislative offices, has helped to further stir up demand. In the 1994 elections, a record number of incumbent legislators left their seats for attempts at higher offices, trying to avoid the newly mandated deadlines for their terms. This left their seats open for city council members, mayors, school board members and other ambitious locals, who in turn vacated their own seats for a shot at the big time. "Term limits are the biggest bonanza for campaign con-sultants ever. They guarantee a fresh crop of prospects," O'Hara says.

And then there is the arms race aspect of politics. "You must be able to match what the other person is doing," says Moore, the Contra Costa County supervisorial candidate. "I would prefer to keep it at a volunteer plane but I don't think that's possible any more."

That may be true. But as some local candidates are already starting to learn, the edge they get from professional help diminishes when their opponents are doing the same thing. When mailboxes become cluttered with political ads, even a narrowly targeted mailing loses some of its power to persuade. Webb, who traces her original victory in part to her use of cable television ads, says that strategy is no longer as effective. "In the last election cycle two years ago, some of the candidates started using television ads," she said. "It didn't work as well for them as it did for me, because I was the only one doing it."

While cable ads may become ubiquitous, and mailboxes overstuffed with political ads, the technology moves on. In the near future of 500-channel television and interactive entertainment, enterprising campaign consultants will undoubtedly find new ways to slip their candidates' names into voters' homes and minds. These tactics will in their turn become obsolete, but one thing is certain: When the professionals move in, there's no turning back. 🏛

The New California: Facing the 21st Century

2nd Edition

The Sacramento Bee's well-known political correspondent, Dan Walters, completed a 9,000 mile odyssey through California's 58 counties which served as the basis for this book. It describes the socioeconomic future of the nation's largest state and political implications of these trends. This 1992 edition is 186 pages long and contains numerous charts with detailed political and demographic data based on the 1990 Census. With an introduction by Larry L. Berg. 5 1/2 X 8 1/2.

Price$11⁹⁵

Bye-bye, GOP. Ta-ta, Dems.

California voters flee traditional parties

Reprinted from *California Journal*, November 1993

Illustration by Chris Van Overloop

By Chris Collett

A favorite topic of debate among political pundits, pollsters and politicians over the last few years has been the question of whether California is more Republican or Democratic in its partisan beliefs. Without much question, it is agreed that the 1970s wasthe decade of the Democrats. In the fallout from Watergate, Jerry Brown was swept in for two terms as governor, and the Democrats built staggering majorities in both houses of the Legislature.

The 1980s, many then argued, belonged to Republicans. Bolstered by the California-based presidency of Ronald Reagan, a two-term governor in George Deukmejian and seat gains in the Assembly, the GOP overtook the Democrats in partisan identification for the first time in 1986. Presumably, as its supporters and some non-partisans have strongly argued, the only thing that kept Republicans from winning majorities in the Legislature and in the state's congressional

Chris Collet is a PhD candidate in political science at the University of California, Irvine.

delegation was gerrymandered districts. By 1987, Secretary of State March Fong Eu had warned her fellow Democrats that "California had become a Republican state."

With this in mind, it seems natural to ask, "To whom does California belong in the 1990s?" Recent election results suggest that the Democrats have re-emerged. Victories in two crucial U.S. Senate races in 1992, and stunning gains in congressional and Assembly seats despite districts more favorable to Republicans suggest that the Democrats, indeed, may be regaining the strength they enjoyed before the Reagan Revolution.

But the answer to the question, surprisingly, is that the decade of the 1990s seems to belong to neither Republicans or Democrats. The '90s, rather, are poised to be the decade of independents, decline-to-states and an assortment of third parties. Beginning in 1968, California steadily drifted from the two major parties, to the point where, in November 1992 (see Graph 1), nearly 14 percent of its voters were registered either as decline-to-state or with one of the state's minor parties. In terms of raw numbers, decline-to-state and minor-party registation have grown at whopping rates of 566 percent and 145 percent respectively since 1968. By comparison, Republican registration has grown at 62 percent and Democratic at 58 percent over the same time period.

Some would argue that in the candidate-centered age of politics, party registration means very little. In fact, recent research by Ed Constantini and Charles Dannehl at the University of California, Davis, has underscored this, by showing the decline in the relationship between Democratic registration and Democratic vote share in California. Furthermore, reg-

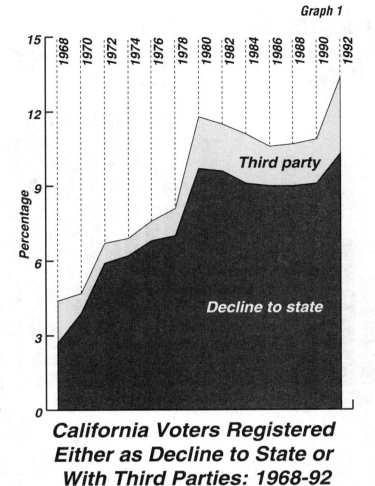

Graph 1

California Voters Registered Either as Decline to State or With Third Parties: 1968-92

source: Secretary of State, Report of Registration 1968-1992

istration data have been considered suspect because it is thought that one to two million voters still on the rolls are "deadwood" — those who have either moved or are deceased.

But the gradual movement away from the two major parties in the last 25 years is evident in the more trusted party identification data as well. Since 1966, *The Field Poll* essentially has asked respondents: "Generally speaking, do you think of yourself as a Republican, or Democrat, or what?" As Graph 2 shows (see page 33), the increase in those who give responses other than "Democrat" or "Republican" has steadily increased from 4.4 percent in 1966 to 33.7 percent in 1992. Like minor-party and decline-to-state registration, this trend reached its peak in last year's election.

While arguing that some sort of

enduring shift in partisan loyalties took place in California in the mid-1980s in the direction of Republicans, scholars of California politics such as Constantini, Kay Lawson of California State University, San Francisco, and James Fay of CSU, Hayward, have acknowledged this turn toward independence as manifested by shifts in registration data. But often, as noted above, survey data regarding party identification are cited to support the Republican cause, and indeed the data do support this case. Republicans have made considerable gains. But if party identification data are looked at in terms of the number of voters supporting neither major party rather than in terms of Republicans versus Democrats (Graph 2) we see a trend much more long term and dramatic than any recent shifts in partisanship.

Because California voters have become increasingly independent, such drastic shifts from Republicans in the late 1980s to Democrats in 1992 are not only possible but very likely to reoccur. Since independents — who again comprise anywhere from 15 to 33 percent of the vote depending on how one looks at it — are more susceptible to short-term electoral factors such as economic conditions, campaigns, and advertisements which influence the vote, elections may boil down solely to which campaign spends the most, has the most potent message, and makes the fewest mistakes. Democratic and Republican labels, even in legislative elections, have clearly diminished in value. "Coattails" have become non-existent.

California's move away from Republicans and Democrats is perhaps most apparent by recent trends in voting for

The independent voter

Graph 2

Percentage of California Voters Identifying with Neither Republicans nor Democrats

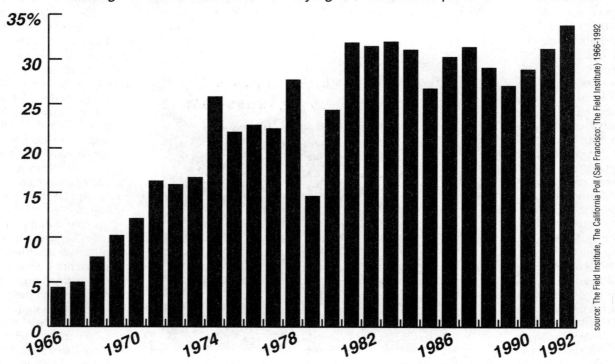

source: The Field Institute, The California Poll (San Francisco: The Field Institute) 1966-1992

third parties. In 1968, when the American Independent and Peace and Freedom parties emerged as the right- and left-wing alternatives to centrist politics during the Vietnam War, voters in California gave minor party candidates for the Legislature and Congress an average of just under 3 percent of the vote. This increaded to nearly 6 percent in 1980, when the Libertarian Party first qualified for the ballot and fielded an entire slate of candidates. By 1990 the average share given to third parties had mushroomed to nearly 7 percent, and passed this mark in Assembly and State Senate races in 1992.

Voting for third-party candidates in statewide elections has also increased substantially. In last year's U.S. Senate races, all third-party votes combined accounted for 7.8 percent in the race between Democrat Dianne Feinstein and Republican John Seymour and 9 percent in the dust-up between Democrat Barbara Boxer and Republican Bruce Herschensohn.

In the presidential race, gadfly independent Ross Perot gained 21.2 percent in the Golden State, which was above his national average.

The question, of course, is whether this increased share of the vote is enough to affect an election. While third parties still are not likely to win any legislative or congressional seats, they still may have an impact on given races. And in recent years, they have definitely impacted several incumbent and aspiring California politicians, including:

• Doug Bosco, a four-term Democratic member of Congress representing the North Coast, who was defeated 43 percent to 42 percent in 1990 by Republican Frank Riggs. Considered by many to be the upset of the year, it was widely held that the Peace and Freedom candidate, Darlene Comingore, who won 15 percent, split the left vote and kept Bosco form retaining his seat.

• Sunny Mojonnier, a four-term Assembly Republican from the San Diego area, who lost by 5 percent to Democrat Dede Alpert in 1990 in a predominant Republican district. While ethics problems and campaign gaffes cost the once popular Mojonnier, Libertarian candidate John Murphy took 11 percent of the vote, and perhaps a close re-election from the Republicans.

• Jeff Marston, another San Diego Republican, lost what was considered a potential Republican seat to Democrat Mike Gotch. In a race that separated Marston from Gotch by 617 votes, Libertarian candidate Ed McWilliams garnered over 5000 votes, or 6 percent;

• Democratic Congressman Richard Lehman, who narrowly retained his seat in 1992 after being challenged by Republican Tal Cloud. In a race that was decided by less than 1000 votes, Peace and Freedom candidate Dorothy Wells received 12 percent, or over 12,000 votes;

• Republican Phil Hawkins who in 1992 challenged incumbent Democratic Assemblyman Bob Epple in the 56th District in Cerritos. Losing to Epple by 1 percent, Hawkins saw Libertarian candidate Richard Gard receive 5 percent of the vote.

• Senator Bill Craven, a Republican who has served in the Legislature since 1973. Running for re-election in 1990 free from a Democratic challenge, Craven still saw over 33 percent of the total votes go to the Peace and Freedom and Libertarian candidates.

In the fall of 1983, John Simon wrote in the *California Journal* that "in only a few cases, does one [of the third parties] hold a balance of power in a legislative or congressional district." But clearly, times have changed. An average of 7 percent — again, the average share given to third parties — was greater than the margin of difference between Republicans and Democrats in 13 legislative and congressional races in 1990, and 18 races in 1992. In total, these 31 seats were distributed nearly evenly to both parties, with Democrats winning 16 and Republicans 15. Thus, if third parties fielded candidates in these competitive, "swing" districts, they could now play a significant role in who wins the seat, and ultimately in determining which party controls each house of the Legislature and the congressional delegation. Because third-party candidates in Assembly races attract a slightly higher average vote share than do their counterparts in state Senate and congressional elections, their impact would likely be the greatest.

Whatever their impact on elections, third parties provide a constant receptacle for disgruntled Californians to cast protest votes. This may be an apt metaphor as a ballot cast for a third party candidacy is often consid-

ered a "wasted" or "throwaway" vote. But with an unpopular governor and Legislature — combined with increasing anxiety about the economy, education and immigration — the third-party phenomenon in California may

be the latest channel of revolt for the politically disgusted. Call it the next chapter in an evolving California story that began in 1978 with Proposition 13 and continued through 1990 and 1992 with stringent term limits and cutbacks in legislative perks, services and salaries.

Equally plausible, however, is that third parties will become a fixture, if not a force, in California politics. No one is suggesting that there will be any Green members of Congress anytime soon, or any Libertarian members of the Assembly. But as long as the aforementioned conditions persist — weak party identification, sluggish economy, dissatisfacation with a government run by both parties — third-party

candidates will continue to attract many voters looking for alternatives. This creates an unpredictable scenario in many districts, especially in north coast areas where the Peace and Freedom Party and Greens have done well, and in Orange and San Diego counties where the Libertarians have prospered. Furthermore, given the trends in statewide party identification and registration and the current electoral climate, it wouldn't be that farfetched to see a Ross Perot or other independent slate of candidates emerge in California politics.

A small path along that route already has been forged by two members of the state Senate — Quentin Kopp of San Francisco and Lucy Killea of San Diego. Both are independents, with Kopp having originally run for the Legislature as an independent and Killea having left the Democratic Party in 1992 to run for re-election as an independent.

Finally, it should be remembered that California has traditionally been an independent state, with a long history of weak parties, non-partisan elections, a knack for quirky and sometime fringe politics and a fondness for eccentric politicians. Where else but California could figures such as Ronald Reagan, Jerry Brown, S.I. Hayakawa, B.T. Collins, Tom Hayden and others garner such attention? The California electorate today is as volatile as ever, and far from moving in one direction or the other as some have argued, it is likely to go both ways, and may, in fact, continue to search for an alternative route. 🏛

Graph 3

Mean Vote Share for Third Party Candidates in Legislative and Congressional Elections: 1966-92

source: Secretary of State, Statement of Vote, 1966-92

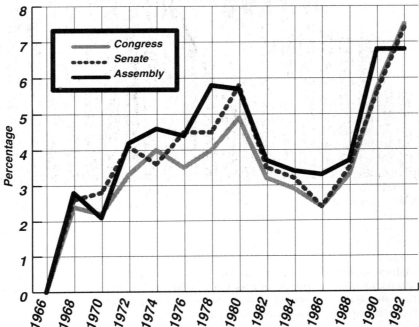

DIRECT DEMOCRACY

In California government the people have three tools that make them very powerful participants in the decision-making process. The initiative, referendum and recall were instituted by Governor Hiram Johnson and the progressives in part to break the hold of the railroad interests on state government in the early 1900's. With all three of the direct democracy devices, a simple majority of those voting determines whether the proposal passes.

• *Initiative*. The initiative gives the people the right to place local or state measures on the ballot if they obtain the required number of signatures. It has also been used by governors, legislators and special-interest groups to get what they want after the Legislature has rejected or been unable to meet their demands. To qualify for the ballot, a statewide constitutional initiative requires signatures equal to eight percent of the vote cast in the last gubernatorial election; initiative statutes require five percent.

After the 1994 gubernatorial election the number of signatures required is:

Constitutional initiative - 693,230
Statutory initiative - 433,269

Today, a powerful and sophisticated initiative industry has developed: signature-gathering firms, pollsters, political lawyers, and campaign management firms specializing in the qualifying and passing of ballot measures.

• *Referendum*. This is a procedure that can be used by the public, if they can gather sufficient signatures, to block a state statute or local ordinance pending a popular vote on the issue. It is not used often, but the threat of a referendum occasionally has the effect of blocking enactment of legislation. This procedure cannot be used to stop urgency bills, and for this reason emergency measures require a two-thirds vote rather than a simple majority in the Legislature. The referendum procedure was used successfully at the statewide level to place four measures the Peripheral Canal and three reapportionment plans — on the ballot in June 1982.

The number of signatures required is the same as for a statutory initiative.

• *Recall*. The third of the Johnson direct-government reforms establishes a petition procedure for placing on the ballot the question of removing any elected official or officials from office. Recall elections are common in local government and have increasingly been used to target state legislators. Former President Pro Tem David Roberti in 1994 and Assembly member Paul Horcher in 1995 had to face voters in recall elections.

California's system of direct democracy does not stop here. The Constitution and local-government charters can be amended only by a vote of the electorate. Neither the state nor any local governmental agency may incur a general-obligation debt without prior approval of the electorate (although revenue bonds can be sold without such approval). At the state level, a simple majority vote is sufficient to approve bond measures for such purposes as higher-education construction, park acquisition and development, the Cal-Vet farm and home program, and water-pollution plants. But at the local level, all bond proposals — even school bonds — require a two-thirds majority.

In recent years, the potency of direct democracy in California has grown. This power was demonstrated by the far-reaching tax revolt, which started with Proposition 13, the Jarvis-Gann property-tax initiative in 1978. This was followed with the "Spirit of 13" spending-limitation measure enacted in 1979, a successful Jarvis-sponsored income-tax indexing proposal in June of 1982, the successful Gann Legislative Reform Initiative of June 1984 and a number of other Proposition 13 follow-up measures thereafter. Proposition 140 imposes term limits on California elected officials, plus it mandates a 38 percent cut in the legislature's budget. Proposition 164 imposes term limits on our U.S. Senators and Members of the House of Representatives. In 1994 two initiatives were at the center of state political debate: The "Three Strikes" (Prop. 184) and illegal aliens (Prop. 187) initiatives. In 1996 the much ballyhooed Civil Rights Initiative abolishing affirmative action programs is likely to be *the* issue of the year. The number of measures qualifying for the ballot shows no sign of abating in the near future.

With these tools, there is hardly any aspect of state government that cannot be controlled by the people.

Signing for fun and profit:

the business of gathering petition signatures

illustration by Wendy Rudick Shaul

BY CHARLES M. PRICE

Reprinted from *California Journal,* November 1992

Well, they're back. After a brief respite from initiative politicking in the June 1992 primary, a small platoon of signature-qualified propositions invaded the November 1992 ballot (Propositions 161-167). While dozens of initiatives were launched by hopeful proponents, only these seven made it.

Why did they succeed where all others failed?

Professional petitioning.

The seven were all jockeyed to ballot status through the efforts of California's only two "out-in-the-streets" signature companies: Kimball Petition Management of Los Angeles, and American Petition Consultants of Sacramento.

All it would have taken for the failed initiatives to qualify was money. Had their backers the money to hire Kimball or American, their proposals, too, would have reached the ballot. Qualifying initiatives using only volunteer activists and shoestring budgets is very difficult. Qualifying an initiative is expensive and lately seems to be the exclusive province of the well-heeled. For instance, according to the secretary of state, 80 percent of the money raised to qualify November's seven initiatives came from contributors giving more than $10,000. (Not only that, the first petition measure to qualify for the June *1994* primary ballot — the school choice or 'voucher' initiative — also used paid petitioners.)

The qualified initiatives and their professional petitioners are:

Charles Price is a professor of political science at California State University, Chico, and a frequent contributor to California Journal.

Prop	Title	Signature Company
161	Assisted Death	American
162	Public Employees Retirement	Kimball
163	Snack Tax Elimination	Kimball
164	Congressional Term Limits	American
165	Budget and Welfare Reform	American
166	Health Care	Kimball
167	State Taxes	Kimball
174	School Choice	American

Brothers Kelly and Fred Kimball Jr. are managing partners of Kimball Petition Managment, which their father founded in the 1960s. While Fred Senior was an arch-conservative who helped qualify many right-wing issues for the ballot (for example, Proposition 6 of 1978, which would have allowed school districts to fire homosexual teachers), Kelly and Fred Junior have shifted their company's ideological focus to more mainstream and even some liberal issues. Thus, in November 1992 the Kimballs worked on petition campaigns for Democratic-leaning interest groups such as state employees, the Tax Reform Association and the California Teachers Association. Since the late 1960s, Kimball has qualified dozens of petitions for state and local ballots.

American Petition Consultants also is the province of two brothers — Mike and Bill Arno. Mike is president, while Bill serves as director of operations. Their firm has qualified mainly Republican-conservative issues over the last decade, however American did qualify the liberal-leaning "Death with Dignity," for this fall. Said Mike Arno, "Philosophically,

I'm opposed to [Proposition 161], but it's a social issue that ought to be decided by the people, not the Legislature."

Despite the fact that they are competitors, competition in the signature-gathering business is not quite like competition in the personal computer business. And the links between the Kimballs and Arnos go back many years. Mike Arno's wife grew up as a neighbor of the Kimballs in Southern California. She persuaded Fred Senior to give Mike his first chance in petitioning as a crew chief for Kimball in the early 1980s, and he learned the business well. Over the years on a few occasions, when deadlines are imminent, Kimball and American have sometimes subcontracted with each other for a certain number of signatures. They've been friendly competitors — until this year.

Clearly, Kimball and American dominate initiative qualifying these days. Between 1982 and 1992 nearly 75 percent (48 of 65) of all of the initiatives on the California ballot have qualified through the efforts of one or the other of these two companies. Once hired, they virtually guarantee their clients' ballot status (each has a nearly a 100 percent success rate). Both firms also earn considerable sums qualifying initiatives in states like Oregon, Nevada, Washington, Michigan, Ohio, Oklahoma and Colorado. And, since the collapse of Communist rule in Eastern Europe, each firm has done consulting work in the newly emerging democracies there. Indeed, another Arno brother, Peter, runs their company's St. Petersburg/Moscow operations, and plans are afoot to establish a new office in Minsk.

Paid petitioning wasn't always needed to get a measure on the ballot in California. In the early years, after the initiative was placed into the state Constitution by reformist Progressives in the 1910s, qualifying could be handled by volunteers because proponents had 150 days to collect fewer than 50,000 signatures — a number based on a certain percentage of the total vote cast for governor at the most recent election (5 percent for a statute; 8 percent for a constitutional amendment).

But as California's population increased massively during the Great Depression and after World War II, collecting and processing the hundreds of thousands of signatures needed within the 150-day circulation period became a logistical nightmare — hence, professional petitioning. And since 1990, when the Colorado Supreme Court refused to review a lower court decision that states could not ban paid petitioning because it limited free speech, paid petitioners have truly come into their own.

Through the early 1980s the paid petitioning process went something like this:

• Kimball or American is contacted by an initiative proponent, and the two sides would settle on a price for collecting a specified number of paid signatures — 100,000 or 200,000, for example, with the remainder usually gathered by volunteers.

• The measure then is submitted to the attorney general's office, which assigns it an official title and summary and looks over the text to make sure it's above board and legal. The attorney general laterals it to the secretary of state's office, which assigns circulation and signature-verification deadlines.

• Thousands of copies of the petition are printed and sent to the Kimball or American crew chiefs around the state.

• Crew chiefs hire reliable solicitors by contacting people from previous campaigns and by advertising for new ones in the classifieds.

• Crew chiefs brief their solicitors on a summary of the main arguments for the initiative and point them toward the best places to find signatures — for instance, shopping centers or where people are waiting in line.

• Crew chiefs also teach solicitors how to persuade a reluctant prospect by saying, "This doesn't mean you agree. It's just to get the measure on the ballot so the people will have a chance to vote on it."

• Solicitors turn in their signatures, receiving 25 to 35 cents per name. Crew chiefs earn 5 to 10 cents for all signatures collected in the city or area.

• Finally, proponents turn their accumulated signatures in to local county clerks for validation and tabulation.

Although paid petitioning in the 1990s follows a similar procedure, there are some interesting new twists in the business.

• **Independent subcontractors:** In the old days, American and Kimball had loyal crew chiefs who worked only for one or the other. But no more. As American's Mike Arno noted, "Today, our crew chiefs [located in most of the state's larger cities] are independent subcontractors. In the old days, we hired a lot of 'mom and pop' operators; for example, housewives who ran petition drives out of their homes. These days our subcontractors all have their own businesses. We try to buy the best contractors available.

"Sometimes, they're ones that have done a lot of Kimball work. These people are free agents and negotiate their best price. So, too, the solicitors are independents. A crew chief says, 'I'll give you 35 cents per signature,' and a solicitor says, 'I want 45 cents, or I won't do it.'"

Moreover, Kelly Kimball noted, "If you're slow in getting signatures, you've got to raise the price for the solicitors. It's a stock market out there. Some circulators will delay turning in their signatures on one of the petitions they're carrying, assuming the price will go up. It never goes down. We raise the price [per signature], and suddenly thousands of signatures come in. They bought low and sold high."

• **Multiple petitions:** To make money in petitioning these days, Kimball and American must have packages of three or four or five initiatives — not merely a single initiative — to entice the best petition subcontractors to work for them. George Gorton, Governor Pete Wilson's campaign manager who was spearheading the governor's budget-welfare reform initiative qualifying effort in 1991, failed in his attempts to negotiate contracts with petition subcontractors. The subcontractors want packages of initiatives because the more petitions, the more money and the better enticement for successful solicitors. In addition, subcontractors prefer to do business with known quantities. Wilson's forces eventually sought out Arno to collect the signatures for what has become Proposition 165.

Said Kimball: "There is no limit to what these people [solicitors] can carry."

Arno, in a similar vein, added: "The most petitions I've ever seen one solicitor handle was 13. He had every initiative ... on an ironing board. People would walk along the board, and he'd say, 'Are you for this one? ... Sign here. This one? ... Sign here. This one?' Some solicitors can make as much as $30 or $40 dollars an hour. Several have made $50,000-$60,000 in a five-month period."

- **Initiative awareness:** Before 1978 and Howard Jarvis' property-tax slashing Proposition 13, the initiative process was not well understood by most interest groups. To attain policy objectives, these groups preferred to concentrate on lobbying and providing campaign contributions to candidates. In the 1990s, however, those same interest groups (and elected officials, as well) are keenly aware of the initiative option, and of the ability of Kimball and American to collect hundreds of thousands of signatures.

However, neither Kimball nor Arno say they try to talk people into filing an initiative — usually. Kimball acknowledged that he put together the Lottery initiative as a pro-active effort. "We were looking for something we could make money on, and somebody who would fund it," Kimball said. "But, there are just too few issues out there like that."

- **Validation:** Another difference between paid petitioning today and yesterday is that the two companies place much more emphasis on collecting *valid* signatures. As Arno explained, "Each of us have computers with lists of all registered voters, and we can do random-sample verifications of signatures brought back by our solicitors. As the petition business has developed, subcontractors don't want to get a reputation for turning in poor work. If they fall below our quality control standard, I can back charge them."

- **Direct mail:** In the early 1980s it looked as if direct-mail companies might supplant street petitioning as the wave of the future. Direct-mail petitioning still is used to supplement some petition drives, but it isn't the main signature source these days. Kimball, more pessimistic than Arno about direct-mail petitioning, warned that direct mail "just flat out doesn't work very well. It worked for Howard Jarvis, and it worked somewhat for [Paul] Gann, but on a limited basis. Many of the people on the Jarvis lists were not young, and some have since died. A direct-mail piece is tremendously expensive. If you don't get a decent contribution return rate, you're spending $10 to $15 to $20 per signature."

- **Motivations of initiative proponents:** On the contemporary scene, initiatives are no longer proposed simply as a last resort by interests failing to get their way in the Legislature. These days some issues are introduced via the initiative process. In addition, some initiatives dealing with the same issue on the same ballot are designed to confuse voters rather than to be approved. Some initiatives are put on the ballot to siphon money from conservative Republicans or liberal Democrats. As a result, the process has become more complicated and Byzantine.

- **The attorney general:** Finally, according to Kimball, the present attorney general, Republican Dan Lungren, has been exceptionally partisan. "The [initiative] summaries his office does contain his political philosophy. They're like campaign literature for the opposition." For instance, attorneys representing proponents of Proposition 167 (the so-called "tax the rich" initiative) had to go to court to get the attorney general's "partisan" summary modified. American's Arno, however, disagrees with Kimball's assessment.

It is still possible for dedicated activists to qualify initiatives in the 1990s, but doing so is a formidable undertaking. Perhaps, the prototype of the idealistic cause/volunteer of petitioning is Ken Masterton of Masterton and Little of Bolinas. Over the last few years, Masterton has directed successful qualification efforts for four different environmental initiatives for the Planning and Conservation League (Proposition 70 of June 1988; Propositions 116 and 117 of June 1990; Proposition 130 of November 1990). In addition, he was successful with Proposition 99 of November 1988 (the tobacco-tax) and Proposition 134 of November 1990 (the alcohol-surtax). While more emphasis is placed on getting volunteer signatures in Masterton's efforts, on most of his petition drives some paid signatures also are collected (indeed, two-thirds of the signatures he collected for Proposition 130 were paid). In addition, to secure his freebie signatures, Masterton must pay coordinators to organize the volunteer solicitors, and it costs thousands just to print all the petitions that will be needed. According to Masterton, the typical volunteer effort to place a statute on the ballot will cost about $250,000 to qualify. Thus, initiative qualifying, even those using mostly volunteer signature collectors, is expensive.

Relations between American and Kimball have cooled recently. The reason: the controversy over the qualification effort for the school-choice, or voucher initiative. Arno was hired by the initiative's proponents to collect the necessary signatures to place the measure on the November 1992 ballot. However, in a unique counter-strategy move, the California Teachers Association hired Kimball as a consultant to work *against* qualification.

"Our strategy in the anti-qualification campaign was to arm the potential signer with the information needed to say 'no,'" said Kimball. "If a well-educated teacher can explain why an initiative is bad to potential signers, this can be very effective. It wouldn't have worked to have our circulators do this. Teachers were ideally suited for it."

Arno, not surprisingly, saw it differently. "On the one hand, you had teachers who saw the choice initiative as a 'life or death' issue and, on the other side, you had people trying to earn money collecting signatures. Many of these people were in agreement with the philosophy of the choice initiative. It's a very frustrating thing to have someone jump in your face when you're trying to collect signatures. We had reports that potential solicitors were offered money not to get signatures, or were threatened if they tried to do so. They used Kelly to locate where all of our people were. If we fail to qualify an initiative, this obviously benefits Kelly."

Both Arno and Kimball are supportive of some reforms to improve the initiative process. Kimball noted, "If it were in my power, I'd really enforce the single-subject rule. I'd also like the system reformed so that voters would be asked a simple question, 'Do you want a state lottery? Yes or no?' And, if a majority of voters say 'yes' then the Legislature would be required to implement the law. We should not have to have voters wade through 20 pages of legal text describing an initiative. People don't have the time or energy for this. My proposal would be a sort of an indirect initiative."

But Arno wants the process to continue. "When I'm invited to speak to college classes," he said, "I always ask this question: 'Were there too many initiatives on the last ballot?' ... 'Which of them would you have like to eliminate from the ballot?' There is always much disagreement on this. 'How many bills were considered by the Legislature last year?' Most think a few hundred. I tell them, 'More than 6000. Can you name five of them?' And, they can't. But they know what the initiatives were. Finally, I ask, 'Who do you trust more — you making the decision or your legislator?' Overwhemingly, *they* want to make the decision." 🏛

initiative reform

Is it time to return to the "indirect" initiative?

Illustration by Mike Tofanelli

By Charles M. Price

Reprinted from *California Journal*, April 1994

I f public attitude toward state government was a radar screen, the little blip marked "confidence" probably has disappeared from view. And the reasons for it are myriad. Corruption unearthed in an FBI sting operation conducted inside the Capitol ensnared legislators, lobbyists and staffers. The economy has been blistered by defense cutbacks, an unemployment rate higher than the national average, a tidal wave of illegal aliens, a never-ending series of fires, floods, drought and earthquakes, and human maelstromes such as

Charles Price is a professor of political science at California State University, Chico, and a frequent contributor to California Journal.

the Los Angeles riots. When dealing with all of this, political institutions often seem mired in gridlock and unable to cope.

Thus, the public took matters into its own hands, using a process of "self-government" established more than 80 years ago — the initiative. Beginning with Proposition 13's overhaul of the property tax system in 1978, voters systematically restructured state political institutions and changed forever the way state and local governments funded themselves. They also put a cap on the amount of time state elected officials may serve in office.

But a growing number of critics feel that the initiative process, set up to curb the influence of special interests on government, has become instead a tool for those interests. Critics also feel that the laws that emerge from the initiative system are flawed. And they want the process overhauled.

The initiative — together with its cousins, the referendum and the recall — first saw the light of day in California back in 1911 when Progressive Governor Hiram Johnson led the charge to write them into the state Constitution. Initiatives allow voters the right, via the petition process, to propose and enact laws and constitutional amendments, and, by so doing, bypass the Legislature and/or governor.

Initiative critics, including elected officials and academicians, point to a number of problems with the current system.

• Initiatives are often authored by special interests or by ambitious politicians, not by average citizens, as Johnson intended.

• These measures are filed and approved for circulation without any in-depth analysis. Although the attorney general makes sure proposals don't violate the constitution, many slip into circulation with drafting errors or are flawed in other ways that must later be sorted out in court.

• Most initiatives qualify for the ballot through the work of professional petition firms rather than the efforts of volunteer citizens.

• Initiative propositions are laden with legalistic jargon, making them difficult to understand for the average voter.

• So-called "counter-initiatives" — two proposals on the same subject and the same ballot — often complicate the voter's ability to sort among conflicting measures.

• Initiatives add to the length of the ballot and number of decisions facing voters.

• Propositions are packaged into deceptive campaigns by slick professional campaign consultants.

• Finally, initiatives, once approved by voters, are amended with great difficulty.

Beyond these problems, a succession of fiscal initiatives have severely hampered the governor and Legislature's ability to provide fiscal leadership — or even craft a budget. Included in this group are Proposition 13's 1978 property tax relief; Proposition 4 of 1979, which imposed government spending limits; Proposition 6 of 1982, which abolished property and gift taxes; Proposition 62 of 1986, which required a two-thirds vote before cities may raise taxes; and Proposition 98 of 1988, which mandated a minimum funding level for K-14 public schools.

Finally, voter adoption of Proposition 140 in November 1990, the harsh term limits and legislative budget reduction initiative, was for many legislators, especially Democrats, the "last straw."

Thus, over the last several legislative sessions, various Democratic legislators have proposed "reforms" to stem the initiative tide: raise the filing fee from $200 to $1000, require that signatures be collected in a specific number of counties, increase the percent of signatures needed to qualify an initiative or require that the percent be geared to registered voters not to the total vote cast for governor at the last election, the current requirment. This proposal would double the number of required signatures (currently 615,958 for a constitutional amendment and 384,974 for a statute). Yet, none of these proposals passed even though Democrats had secure majorities in both houses.

Restrictions on the initiative process fail for a number of reasons. First, conservative Republicans are wary of under-

cutting a process they often have used with great success. Term limits, for instance, was proposed by former Assemblyman and former Los Angeles County Supervisor Pete Schabarum — a Republican conservative. Second, polls repeatedly show that the public supports the initiative process. And although that support has declined over the last several decades, it still is backed by more than 60 percent of the electorate, according to *The Field Poll*. Third, an alliance of interests united to help protect the initiative during the 1991-92 legislative session. This "Initiative Coalition" included political watchdogs such as Common Cause and the League of Women Voters, environmental groups such as the Planning and Conservation League and the Sierra Club, and conservative anti-tax groups such as the Howard Jarvis Taxpayers Association, People's Advocate (founded by the late Paul Gann), and Paul Gann's Citizen Organization. The coalition opposed restricting the initiative process because its members had successfully sponsored initiatives and were reluctant to see the process dismantled. Moreover, the Jarvis and Gann groups have used the initiative process as a money-making tool to help fund their activities.

One significant initiative reform emerged from the 1991-92 session, however — Democratic Assemblyman Jim Costa's ACR 13, which established a 15-member Citizen's Commission on Ballot Initiatives to study the process and propose possible remedies. Under ACR 13's provisions, the governor, Assembly speaker and Senate Rules Committee each selected four members, with appointees a reflection of the state's diverse population. The commission also included a designee of the secretary of state, attorney general and president of the County Clerk's Association. Retired Legislative Analyst A. Alan Post, one of the most respected former officials in the state, was selected to chair the commission.

The commission met periodically during spring 1993 to listen to various initiative experts recommend initiative reforms and to formulate a proposal. Two experts in particular played key roles in framing the commission's deliberations: attorney Robert Stern, former counsel to the Fair Political Practices Commission and author of "California's Fourth Branch of Government;" and Floyd Feeney, a University of California, Davis, law professor and co-author of "Improving the Initiative Process: Options for Change." The "Initiative Coalition" also provided input.

In the end, the initiative process gained a vote of confidence from the commission, although there was substantial consensus that it had some problems. As Post commented, "I don't think that commissioners felt the initiative process should be constrained nor that it was overused. The intent was to make it a better instrument." Post and his colleagues agreed a comprehensive package of initiative reforms was needed and, in January 1994, they presented their recommendations to the Legislature. Costa packaged these recommendations into an omnibus initiative reform bill introduced in February 1994.

The most dramatic change proposed by the commission involves reinstitution of a modified "indirect initiative." Currently, initiatives that qualify go "directly" to the next statewide ballot. The commission would detour those measures by requiring that qualified initiatives first go to the

Legislature for evaluation.

Under an "indirect" system, sponsors of an initiative would have 180 days (30 more than under the current system) to circulate petitions and gather enough signatures to place their proposal on the ballot. But instead of going before voters at the next statewide election, the proposal instead would be sent to the Legislature, which would have 45 days to act on it. Lawmakers would hold hearings where proponents and opponents could testify. Lawmakers also would negotiate with sponsors to iron out flaws or correct drafting errors. Sponsors then could amend the measure as long as the amendments were consistent with the "purposes and intent" of the original proposal. Each house would vote on the initiative and — if the Legislature passed and governor signed it — it would become law without going before voters. The governor and Legislature also could adopt their own law on the same subject, and proponents could choose to withdraw their proposition if satisfied with the effort. If, however, the governor and lawmakers reject a qualified initiative, it automatically would be placed on the next statewide ballot, where it would become law if approved by voters. If a statute, the Legislature subsequently could amend it after three years by a two-thirds vote of each house. Constitutional amendments could not be amended by the Legislature.

There are advantages to this approach, the commission argued. For one, proponents would have a little more time to qualify their petitions, and this might encourage more volunteer rather than paid signature collecting. More important, it would provide a mechanism for revising initiatives after they have been filed. Today, qualified measures go on the ballot, period. The commission's plan, however, would allow for hearings, complete with bill analyses, review and amendments. Oversights, ambiguities and gaffes in the initiative text could be corrected. For example, opponents of Proposition 165, sponsored in 1992 by Governor Pete Wilson to reform welfare and the budget process, focused on one significant drafting error: Although the proposal gave the governor emergency fiscal powers, the Legislature was not given the power to override his decisions. George Gorton, Governor Wilson's initiative campaign manager, admitted to the drafting flaw but contended the courts would take care of it. This could have been avoided had the commission's format been in force because Wilson would have had the opportunity to amend his proposal.

There are problems with the commission's recommendations, however. Hiram Johnson sought a procedure that would bypass a gridlocked or special interest-dominated Legislature. The proposal puts the Legislature back in the loop. Also, from 1911 to 1966, the California Constitution included both a direct and an indirect initiative, but the latter device was rarely used. Finally, *The Field Poll* reported in 1990 that 50 percent of Californians opposed the indirect initiative, while only 41 percent favored it. Also, if initiatives never reached the ballot, it would mean less money-making opportunities for campaign consultants.

In addition, opponents often want proposals killed, not amended, and see their best chance at the ballot. In this vein, they might not want to tip off proponents to drafting errors at a legislative hearing but would rather spring these shortcomings on proponents later in the campaign.

The Post Commission also included a smorgasbord of other fine-tuning reforms, including additional contribution disclosure statements, improved signature-verification procedures, better ballot design, and full disclosure of the top five contributors to the proposition.

The commission, however, did not deal with the role of money in the initiative process. Court rulings mostly have preempted the subject. Powerful groups like the California Teachers' Association or the tobacco industry are in a better position to qualify their proposals than is, say, an animal rights' group because wealthy organizations can spend a lot of money on professionals to collect the required number of signatures. The U.S. Supreme Court ruled in 1988 in *Meyers v. Grant* that states can not prohibit paid petitioning because the ban limits free speech.

Clearly, the side with the most campaign money, particularly if it's by more than a two-to-one or three-to-one margin, has a better chance of winning at the ballot box. This advantage is even more enhanced in the 1990s because the "fairness doctrine" — which once required radio and television stations to provide some free air time to proponents or opponents of propositions with modest financial resources — is, at present, dead. Yet courts also have ruled that attempts to set contribution or expenditure limits also violate free speech.

The contemporary initiative process seems to work. Since the 1970s, only about 20 percent of the filed initiatives actually qualified for the ballot. Of these, only about one-third were approved by voters. If "too many" initiatives get on the ballot, or if initiatives are too lengthy or complex, voters tend to play it safe and vote "no." Thus, in effect, the initiative process already has a self-correcting mechanism.

For his part, Costa has pushed ahead with plans to author legislation to implement some commission recommendations. At the end of February, the Fresno lawmaker introduced AB 3181, which incorporates those recommendations that received unanimous support from the commission. Among the bill's provisions are the requirement for legislative hearings on proposed initiatives, a procedure for proponents to amend their measures, an extension of the circulation period, an improved signature-verification system, and provisions for additional campaign statements.

Costa also introduced ACA 40, which puts provisions of AB 3181 before voters. Both bills are headed for their debut before the Assembly Elections and Reapportionment Committee. Randall Henry, a senior consultant to Costa, expressed guarded optimism about the fate of the two bills, saying that Costa packaged only those recommendations that had been given unanimous approval by the commission, with its varied representation.

Still, Costa's success could depend on how lawmakers perceive declining public support for the initiative, legislative anger over term limits and support from the Initiative Coalition.

Meanwhile, the public seems to be in for a breather — the June 1994 ballot contains only one initiative. 🏛

In the shadow of Jarvis and Gann

Citizen initiators tilt at the electoral windmill

By Charles M. Price

Reprinted from *California Journal*, April 1995

Seventeen years ago, a singular success turned their names into household words, made them instant inductees into the grass-roots hall of fame, secured their places in California political history and launched a movement that even today has the power to turn normally forthright, sane and otherwise stalwart politicians into quivering mounds of Jell-O. One was a cantankerous Southern Californian, the other a gentlemanly Sacramentan, and prior to their success, they had a somewhat checkered history as authors and proponents of ballot initiatives. Both separately and together, they had logged a record of failure that might have caused ordinary mortals to develop a more rewarding hobby.

But these two had the kind of genuis that comes from the dogged pursuit of a singular goal. Or, maybe they just had blind luck, for in 1978, Howard Jarvis and Paul Gann hit paydirt, nirvanah, the promised land. They offered up a property tax relief initiative that captured the imagination of beleaguered taxpayers, who endorsed their proposal — known then and forever as Proposition 13 — and made it the law of the land. From that day forward, Jarvis and Gann became mythical practitioners of initiative politics.

Jarvis and Gann scored a huge success, but many less-successful promoters push their ideas just as doggedly — often in the face of defeat after defeat.

Take, for instance, Robert W. Wilson, a Southern California artist and initiative proponent whose motto might well be, "If at first you don't succeed — try, try again." In 1964 Wilson qualified a ballot initiative that would have set up a statewide lottery — Proposition 16 that year. Voters, however, rejected it.

"I was 20 years too early," Wilson lamented, adding that Nevada gambling interests and California horsetracks poured millions of dollars into the effort to derail his initiative because they feared the competition for gambling dollars.

Embittered by his experience, Wilson in 1965 filed a new initiative that would have allowed casino-style gambling in Adelanto, a small San Bernardino County community in the Mojave Desert a few hours drive from Los Angeles. It also would have provided for extended pari mutuel wagering on horse racing. The initiative was a less-than-subtle swipe at the enemies of Proposition 16, but Wilson failed to gather enough signatures to qualify it for the ballot. Undaunted, Wilson has resubmitted his Adelanto gambling measure 25 times since 1965. It has yet to qualify.

Wilson and his band of allies remain undaunted. "Do you realize that Californians spend over $3.5 billion yearly gambling in Nevada?" asked John Brown, an Oxnard attorney who co-authored Wilson's 1994 gambling proposal. "That's why Nevada doesn't have to have a state income tax. Hang Nevada."

Brown may be correct, and a whole bunch of Californians may agree with him. But the act of qualifying

---

Charles M. Price is a professor of political science at California State University, Chico, and a frequent contributor to California Journal.

an initiative requires more than an idea whose time may have come. It requires big money. Thus far, Wilson and Brown have been unable to find the financial backing needed to hire professionals such as American Petition Consultants to secure the needed signatures. If they ever do find a bankroll, they might just qualify their idea. And given the mood of the electorate, it might pass. After all, that's precisely what happened to those old men of myth — Jarvis and Gann.

Meanwhile, Robert W. Wilson symbolizes the potentials and pitfalls of the initiative process. In a nutshell, the process that has so enmeshed Wilson goes like this:

A person or group drafts an initiative idea — whether a statute or constitutional amendment — into the proper legal form. Generally speaking, politically savvy proponents rely on experienced attorneys to put their proposals into proper legalese. Others may request drafting assistance from the legislative counsel if the request is accompanied by the signatures of 25 voters. The Legislative Counsel's Office lends this assistance as time permits. The proponent then submits the initiative proposal to the attorney general, along with a $200 deposit for processing costs that will be refunded if the measure qualifies. The Attorney General's Office gives the proposal a title and summary, after which it is sent to the Secretary of State's Office, which sets the deadline for turning in enough valid signatures to qualify for the ballot — currently, 432,945 for statutes and 692,711 for constitutional amendments. In addition, a fiscal analysis is prepared by the Department of Finance and Joint Legislative Budget Committee. Finally, if a sufficient number of valid signatures are collected by the deadline, the measure goes on the next statewide ballot where voters approve or reject it.

Over the last 30 years, initiatives have increasingly occupied center-stage in California politics. Among the most prominent were Proposition 4 — the Political Reform Act of November 1974; Jarvis-Gann's Proposition 13 of June 1978; Proposition 140 and its imposition of legislative term limits in November 1990; Proposition 174's school-voucher proposal of June 1993; and Propositions 184 and 187 of 1994, better known as the "three strikes" and "illegal immigration" initiatives. Already approved for the March 1996 primary election is an "open primary" initiative that would allow voters the right to vote for any primary candidate regardless of party label. In addition, another school-voucher bombshell is in the works, also aimed at March 1996, while a measure to abolish the state's affirmative-action laws could land on the November 1996 ballot. All three promise to have substantial impact on the elections of 1996. Overall, since 1964, nearly 650 initiatives have been filed in California, approximately 17 percent have qualified for the ballot and about 7 percent approved by voters.

Initiative qualifying may have crested in the 1987-90 period when some 36 made it to the ballot. Of these, 15 were approved. Since 1990, the number of proposals qualifying for the ballot seems to have slacked off despite a continued stream of petitions circulated for signatures.

What sort of people file initiatives? Essentially, there are three types: elected officials, executives of financially powerful interest groups and private citizens. Most initiatives that qualify for the ballot are authored by the first two groups. These proponents are politically astute and often have the financial wherewithall necessary to promote petition drives. They nearly always hire professional firms to guarantee their measures make the ballot.

Elected officials have introduced a fair share of initia-tives over the past three decades as well. In particular, conservative Republican officeholders such as John Schmitz, John Briggs, Pete Schabarum, Floyd Wakefield, Don Rogers, Frank Hill, Bill Dannemeyer and Ross Johnson have put forward ideas and, by so doing, have sought to bypass the Legislature, which has been controlled for the most part by liberal Democrats.

Not that Democrats, too, haven't felt compelled to use the ballot. The likes of former Assemblymen Lloyd Connelly and Dick Floyd and Senator Tom Hayden and former Senator Alan Robbins have filed initiatives. A more recent trend has been for major statewide officeholders or candidates to propose initiatives as adjuncts to their campaigns. John Van De Kamp, Leo McCarthy, George Deukmejian, Pete Wilson and March Fong Eu are examples. Interest-group leaders such as John Henning of the AFL-CIO, Kirk West of the Chamber of Commerce and Carol Lee of the California Medical Association have been active initiative proponents as well.

Even political insiders frequently fall short in their signature-qualifying efforts, however. For example, no one is more keenly aware of the problems in collecting sufficient valid signatures in the right amount of time than the secretary of state. Yet, former Secretary of State Eu failed to qualify her "Dimes Against Crimes" initiative in 1987.

It was average citizens like Robert Wilson, not political insiders, whom Progressives wanted to empower when they first placed the initiative procedure into the state Constitution not long after the turn of the century. After all, elected officials and lobbyists had access to the formal institutions of lawmaking — Legislature and governor. The initiative was designed for those outside the regular process.

Who are these average Joes and Janes? And why are they willing to plunk down $200 for their initiative idea? How do they hope to collect the hundreds of thousands of signatures needed to place their measure on the ballot?

Some private-citizen initiators believe strongly in their issue but have little appreciation or understanding of the costs of printing thousands of petitions and coordinating a massive signature drive. For example, builder Norman Bedford of Healdsburg was the subject of several expensive lawsuits. Bedford became angered by what he considered to be excessive costs for attorneys, and he filed an initiative to limit their fees.

"I thought I would receive financial support from the insurance industry with my proposal," Bedford admits. But, the money never appeared. He has filed seven initiative proposals over the years, but none has ever qualified.

In 1973, in a one-week period, Patrick O'Shaughnessy of San Francisco filed 20 separate initiatives on a wide variety of subjects. None qualified, and O'Shaughnessy was out $4000 for his trouble. And, in 1994 one proposed initiative on "Forfeiture of Office" listed an all-time high of 57 co-authors. It, too, failed to make the ballot.

Some citizens launch initiatives aware that qualifying them will be difficult but do so to get media coverage for their measure, or to give their issue legitimacy. For example, Barton Gilbert, in the 1970s and '80s, and currently Jack Herer have promoted efforts to legalize marijuana under certain circumstances — an issue the Legislature has been reluctant to take on. None has ever made the ballot.

Said Robert Wilson, "I didn't even try to qualify many of my [gambling] initiatives. I kept reintroducing them because this was my idea — my way of maintaining a kind of patent on the idea."

A fair number of private-citizen initiatives are filed because particular interests such as doctors, lawyers, teachers or insurance companies have a virtual veto over hostile legislation. Thus, to circumvent the power these groups hold over the Legislature, proponents resort to initiatives such as single-payer state health system, school vouchers or "pay at the pump" no-fault auto insurance.

Illustration by Mike Tofanelli

Some citizen initiatives promote non-traditional approaches to government. Some of those filed over the last two years:

Matt Dillon proposes a 24-hour-a-day, 365-days-a-year telephone voting system on propositions submitted to voters.

Former Alaska Senator Mike Gravel would allow California citizens a chance to participate in a world constitutional convention to establish global governance. It appropriates 25 cents per California resident from the general fund to help finance the effort.

Cheryl Fort wants to amend the preamble to the state's Constitution.

Norman Bedford wants to implant facial identifying numbers subcutaneously on released violent felons.

Robert Bell proposes that California secede from the Union and become an independent nation.

Eurica Californiaa wants laws on nudity to apply to males and females equally, bare chests and all.

Occasionally, initiatives sponsored by private citizens have qualified. In the 1970s Ed and Joyce Koupal, after failing to qualify a recall of Governor Ronald Reagan, left Sacramento and moved to signature-rich Los Angeles. Activists — mainly students and housewives — were organized into the People's Lobby, a petition-sponsoring group that promoted

liberal causes. With minimal financial resources but dedicated volunteers and a no-nonsense approach to gathering signatures, they succeeded in qualifying several of their initiatives. Ironically, one novice who learned at their knee was Howard Jarvis, himself a right-wing ideologue.

And then there were Jarvis and Gann. Prior to Proposition 13, Jarvis and Gann had failed to qualify any of their six initiatives. After Proposition 13, they jointly or separately succeeded in qualifying a number of measures, with several winning voter approval. They also established two organizations that promote conservative causes via the ballot box.

The most-recent heir-apparent to the Jarvis-Gann legacy is Mike Reynolds, a Fresno native whose 18-year-old daughter was murdered by a paroled felon after she refused to give him her purse. Reynolds labored for years to pass stiffer penalties for violent felons, only to see his effort crushed in a Democrat-dominated Legislature. In 1993, Reynolds went the initiative route — his cause helped when Petaluma 12-year-old Polly Klaas was kidnapped and murdered by an ex-con with a history of violent crime. His proposal became the "three strikes and you're out" initiative of 1994 — Proposition 184.

In addition, public-interest lobby groups with modest financial resources — for example, Common Cause, the American Cancer Society, Campaign California and Californians Against Waste — using mostly dedicated volunteer signature collectors have sometimes been able to qualify petitions. Another, the California Planning and Conservation League, has enlisted high-powered and high-paying allies to fund its initiatives, mostly by writing shares of the spoils into the initiative on behalf of those it seeks as co-sponsors. This "Christmas tree" approach has succeeded in qualifying and passing ballot measures in the 1990s. In addition, the Ross Perot-inspired United We Stand, led by state chair Kirk McKenzie, attempted to qualify four separate initiative proposals in 1994 but failed.

Much of the criticism concerning ballot-box lawmaking — use of counter-initiatives; paid signature-gathering; partisan game-playing; and expensive, duplicitous campaigns — can be tied to elected officials and financially powerful interest groups who seem able to buy their way onto the ballot at a whim. But it is the Howard Jarvises, Paul Ganns and Robert Wilsons of the world — underfunded grass-roots citizens or groups with altruistic, irksome, wacky, innovative, naive or even unconstitutional proposals — that more closely reflect what Progressives had in mind when they advanced the initiative process nearly a century ago. 🏛

LOCAL GOVERNMENT

One reason why Californians have so many elections and frequently such long ballots is that the state has a complex system of local government. Every citizen in the state probably is a resident of a dozen or more units of local government, among them:

Counties. The state has 58 counties (counting San Francisco), some of which are governed by general state law and others by charters (similar to constitutions) voted by the people.

Cities. Most Californians live in one of the state's 470 cities, but some live in unincorporated areas in which municipal services are provided by the county and special districts. General law cities (384) operate through a structure established by state law. Charter cities have more flexibility in their structure and procedures.

City-county. San Francisco is a combined city and county operating under a charter.

School districts. Public schools from kindergarten through 12th grade are operated by independent districts with directly elected governing boards. There are about 1200 school districts in the state.

Community college districts. Directly elected trustees also run community colleges, which provide freshman and sophomore courses.

Special districts. These can vary from large regional districts such as the Metropolitan Water District in Los Angeles to a local mosquito-abatement district. There are more than 3400 special districts formed to provide specific services for a defined area. Most directors are elected by the public.

Local Agency Formation Commissions. Each county has a commission that serves as clearinghouse for annexation of territory by a local agency and for formation of new cities.

Regional governments. There are no all-powerful regional governments in California, but there are numerous limited-purpose regional agencies such as the Bay Area Air Pollution Control District, Rapid Transit District and Sewer Service Agency. Efforts have been underway for years to enact a powerful regional government for the San Francisco area. There are several voluntary associations of local governmental agencies designed to help resolve regional problems; these include the Association of Bay Area Governments and the Southern California Association of Governments.

City and county government

Counties are run by boards of supervisors elected by the public, usually by district. In most counties, the board appoints an administrative officer to supervise the details of county government. Counties also have other directly elected officials, such as the district attorney, the sheriff and the assessor.

Cities are operated under a variety of systems. Under one basic arrangement not widely used, the strong-mayor system, the mayor is the chief-administrative officer of the city, and policy is set by the council. The more common system establishes the mayor, who may be elected either by the people or by the council, as the ceremonial chief of the city and puts the administration of municipal affairs under the control of a powerful city manager or administrator. The council has the power to appoint and remove the manager. Under this council-manager form of government, the council is supposed to be limited to the setting of policy, but there have been a few cases in which a mayor, by virtue of a strong personality, had been able to run the city government, relegating the manager to the role of errand boy.

More frequently, however, the manager, by virtue of the fact that he is a full-time employee with a large staff, plays a role as large as or even greater than the council in establishing policy.

Special districts are usually administered by a superintendent, general manager or other executive selected by the governing board. 🏛

The local government lament

Funding crises plague strapped counties, cities in fight for fiscal survival

By Nancy H. Martis

Reprinted from *California Journal*, November 1994

Illustration by Norm Hines

When Merced County finished budgeting its revenues for the year, it became a local government imprisoned. With 90 percent of its money going to state-mandated programs and services, the county simply ran out of funds. In short, there was no remaining 10 percent to budget toward the operation of the county.

When we had taken a breakdown that takes health and welfare, the judicial system, then local public safety under the new maintenance-of-effort requirement into consideration, our revenues were locked up," said Clark Channing, chief administrative officer for Merced County. The county found itself in need of at least $6 million just to meet its operational obligations through the end of the year. Seven other counties — Butte, Del Norte, Humboldt, Lassen, Mendocino, Siskiyou and Yolo — were in a similar fix, locked into funding specific services and coming up short thanks to their jailer, the state.

Within the last month, counties have been handed a rough sentence. Governor Pete Wilson's actions during the last week of September were significant for the state's financially strapped local governments, particularly counties. He signed into law the county-feared — yet inevitable — AB 2788 by Assemblyman Willie Brown Jr. (D-San Francisco), which requires local governments to maintain a public safety funding level, or "maintenance of effort," equal to the previous year in order to receive monies from the state's half-cent sales tax, authorized under Proposition 172 in 1992. Two days later, he vetoed a one-time county bail out measure that would have shifted to eight counties — including Merced —

a total of almost $14 million in property tax revenue earmarked for schools.

It's the county lament: nearly 90 percent of all services run at the county level are state-mandated programs. Counties serve as "agents of the state" in administering more than 250 different kinds of programs, an obligation resulting from the state constitution and its statutes. The county is responsible for the "social well-being" of its residents, providing law and order on the streets, a court system, a county jail system and basic food assistance, among other things such as development. Yet because of these so-called "Big M" mandates, county boards of supervisors generally lack policy discretion over mandated minimum service levels. Therefore, the more mandates, the tighter the fiscal constraints.

"We are truly under siege right now," said Dave Oppenheim, senior legislative analyst for the California State Association of Counties. Since 1992, the state has shifted $2.6 billion in property tax monies away from counties and directed it to schools, as required by voter-approved Proposition 98, passed in 1988. The merits of securing dollars for education aside, Oppenheim says that because the state's 58 counties are locked into funding state mandated programs or services — which ties up 90 percent of their budgets — the remaining 10 percent in discretionary funds leaves little or no room for improvements.

According to the state controller's office, which keeps the authoritative record of expenditures and revenues for California's counties, the property tax comprises the largest single portion of revenue. In 1991-92, for example, property taxes accounted for $5.7 billion, or 22.6 percent, of county revenue. Two years and two property tax shifts later, it was minus $2.6 billion, a huge blow to counties' ability to finance themselves along with their profusion of mandated programs.

Cities, on the other hand, have discretion over their entire budgets and are able to identify and allocate funds according to their various priorities, although cities, too, are strapped. Counties have begun over the past few years to complain that they shoulder more of the burden for social costs and suggest cities must pick up some of the slack for such things as booking fees in jails and the costs of health and welfare. One city policy expert who declined to be identified acknowledged that the relationship between cities and counties is almost marriage-like. "The arguments we have are fiscal," the source said. "One of the biggest problems we face is that cities and counties do not work with each other. The county's goal lately has been to portray cities as being really, really wealthy and to bring [cities] down to their level, but we need to figure out a way we can make everyone better."

So where does the solution lie? A new Constitutional Revision Commission has been formed under Wilson and has been meeting over the past five months. It is charged with the task of evaluating and recommending fundamental changes to the constitution, all for the betterment of modern-day government's functions. Wilson noted in his veto message of the county bailout bill, "I remain convinced that the state and counties must work together to restructure our fiscal and program structures so that counties have the responsibility and ability to manage their resources and program priorities. It is more than regrettable that supervisors do not have more flexibility to set their own local priorities."

But the city expert queries, "Do you think the way to get cities and counties to stop fighting is to put it in the constitution? That sounds pretty rigid to me."

Some counties have toyed with the idea of actually seeking funding solutions, only to find themselves in court defending their creativity. One such example is a first-of-its-kind ballot proposal in Sacramento. Voters are scheduled to decide November 8th on a half-cent sales tax to benefit public safety, which includes law enforcement, children safety and adult mental health. If the measure gets two-thirds voter approval, the expected $57 million the tax would generate could be earmarked for law enforcement, courts and protective services; with a simple majority, the money would go into the general fund. A lawsuit filed at the end of August by the Howard Jarvis Taxpayers Association made an unsuccessful attempt to block the measure from the ballot, claiming that it violated the state constitution's single subject rule; however, even if it passes, a court challenge is inevitable.

Other counties desperate to raise revenues have experienced similar dilemmas with voter-approved tax increases, passing them with a majority vote and then being challenged in court by anti-tax groups, which have prevailed recently in Monterey, Santa Clara and San Diego counties. Courts have followed the Supreme Court decision of *Rider v. San Diego County*, which prohibits an entity from operating as a county body to provide services and try to "make up" for funds lost due to reduced property taxes without the benefit of a two-thirds vote.

With such foreboding legal challenges, getting creative to raise revenue is increasingly difficult for local government. Yet many are taking a stab at other funding solutions, such as public-private partnerships and benefit assessments, all of which Peter Detwiler of the Senate Local Government Committee says are "absolutely crucial in the absence of major structural reform. The demand for public service didn't decrease, but voters have walled off certain actions and the Legislature has walled off certain fees. When Proposition 13 passed, they didn't say 'no parks,' they said, 'You don't get the money.'" Other sources, such as sales taxes, parking fines and license fees, account for a small portion of local county revenue since big-ticket revenue generating operations usually are within incorporated city limits.

Far from resolved, the subject surrounding local government and its financing and the question of restructuring is hot and near-desperate, as evidenced by the plethora of reports on local government woes. One such analysis was compiled by the Senate Local Government Committee following an interim hearing in December on local revenue increases. Entitled "Public Revenues, Public Awareness," the report summarizes conclusions from the hearing that indicates general agreement on maintaining public facilities and protecting citizens from overtaxation. Yet within the Capitol, throughout the cities and counties, there is resounding agreement over at least one concept that sounds cliche but is in all likelihood the only hope: To free government from its fiscal handcuffs, all forms must work together. Otherwise, the city policy expert foresees, "We'll all be incompetent and unpopular." 🏛

California JOURNAL

Independent analysis of politics and government

25 Years of Reporting Excellence

- Each month California Journal brings its readers lively, non-partisan reporting on the politics, people, and issues at the cutting edge of the nation's leading state.
- In addition to each month's lively coverage, subscribers receive the Roster, an award-winning listing of all elected and appointed state officials, and Ballot Booklets, analyses of all ballot measures written in clear understandable language.

Subscribe Today

Subscriptions to California Journal are $34.95 per year. Send your order to California Journal 2101 K Street, Sacramento, California 95816. Or, for faster service, Fax your order to (916) 446-5369 or call (916) 444-2840.

1970 25 1995
Public Service Journalism

OrangeCounty

Illustration by Mike Tofanelli

Fiscal disaster savages once-wealthy county, but the wounds were self-inflicted

By Nancy H. Martis

Reprinted from *California Journal*, February 1995

Perhaps Roseann Rosannadanna said it best: "It just goes to show ya, it's always something." The character portrayed by the late comedienne Gilda Radner probably wasn't referring to the wide array of disasters that have been visited on California. And she certainly wasn't referring to the most recent financial catastrophe — the Orange County investment fiasco that has set national records as the largest county government disaster in history. But Orange County's travail brings Radner's catchphrase to mind.

The mid-1970s were no golden days in Orange County. Rocked by scandal, disgraced by indictments and paralyzed with fear, this bastion of conservatism faced a long, rough road to recovery following near-mortal wounding suffered in that decade. Twenty years ago, then-Orange County District Attorney Cecil Hicks spearheaded an investigation into corrupt development dealings that resulted in no less than 43 indictments, targeting congressmen, supervisors, special interest lobbyists and others. Hicks obtained at least 33 convictions, prompting political scientists to designate Orange County as "one of the most corrupt places in the country" and citizens' groups to launch political-reform efforts aimed at blocking any possible recurrence of the type of corruption the county was forced to survive.

What led to the county's troubles, *California Journal* reported in December 1977, "was that the county grew fast and furiously, more than doubling in population between 1960 and [1977], from 703,000 to 1.8 million... It has burgeoned into a scarcely distinguishable succession of sprawling tracts. And as the orange groves, bean fields and strawberry patches were replaced by streets and gutters, driveways and houses, political degeneration set in." That degeneration took the form of voter apathy — local city council election turnout averaged between 12 percent and 19 percent — and special-interest infiltration.

Although Orange County's current financial catastrophe is not the result of political corruption, some suggest that perhaps the county never fully convalesced following the charges and convictions that infested it in the mid-1970s. Earnest efforts were under way to prevent further political corruption, as in the "Time Is Now, Clean Up Politics" (TINCUP) drive, but the county's recovery addressed only its symptoms. In other words, it may be cleaner than the it was in the 1970s, but now it's broken.

The news of the once-wealthy county's financial demise came in two waves in December. First was the surprise resignation on Monday, December 5th, of Orange County Treasurer-Tax Collector Robert L. Citron, who had held the office for 24 years, managing the $18.5 billion investment fund. Citron's risky investment practices paid off big for years, earning average returns of 8 percent to 10 percent. But his strategy of using $12 billion in securities as collateral for short-term loans, an approach federal Securities Exchange Commission officials are calling improper, relied on interest rates remaining flat or dropping. Last year's sharp rise in interest rates, however, threw the fund off, and Citron disclosed that the investment pool lost $1.5 billion in 1994, bad news for the county and the 180 other public agencies with money nvested in the same pool. The losses now are estimated at $2.02 billion. The SEC had begun investigating the fund's portfolio just

days before Citron resigned.

Then came the second shock wave. The Orange County Board of Supervisors spent all day Tuesday, December 6th, behind closed doors, juggling options to protect the county from sure disaster. At 5:01, in a rare move of last resort, the county filed for federal bankruptcy protection. Fearing a run on the fund, supervisors reportedly felt this was their only option given the seizure earlier in the day by CS First Boston Corporation of $2 billion of the county's securities used as collateral for its loans.

At the center of the controversy has been Citron's use of "derivatives," a term widely used since Orange County's troubles first surfaced. Citron entered into what are called "reverse repurchase agreements," or deals that use securities as collateral to borrow more money for investment in other securities. According to Sacramento City Treasurer Tom Friery, state law permits local governments to enter these agreements to supplement the interest income normally received from investment securities already owned. Friery, who does not participate in high-risk investment practices, explained, "These agreements result in short-term transactions of five-30 days where an owner of investment securities temporarily sells and agrees to buy back the securities in exchange for cash and an agreement to pay interest to the cash lender for the short time period. The original owner then takes the cash and buys another short-term investment security to coincide with the agreement."

According to Friery, Citron apparently used $7 billion to buy investment securities, which he then used as collateral to borrow close to $7 billion in an arrangement where a rate of interest was fixed for 30 days. Citron, however, did not purchase short-term investment securities, but long-term securities that had fixed interest rates. In such a case, the investor stands to make a lot of money if interest rates go down; but he or she may lose if they go up. When interest rates rose, the value of the derivatized bonds plummetted, and the borrowing cost to Orange County soared. Citron allegedly did this three times and wound up with a $22 billion portfolio, more than $14 billion of it leveraged against the original $7 billion.

As investigators, legislators and political operatives sift through the

tons of documents relative to Orange County's once-mighty investment portfolio, a theme similar to one that surfaced in the '70s is cropping up once again: The government structure in the third most-populous county in the state is flawed, that Orange County is a community without a nucleus, without a leader and therefore without a system of accountability; in other words, one that actually invites lax governance, particularly when it comes to elected officials supervising other elected officials. Governmental experts are beginning to develop proposals to address these flaws.

Questions over whether the county's structure invited financial problems have yet to be answered since the situation itself still is unfolding, although there is already much support for some form of restructuring. "Orange County is a rootless political system because they have no dominant city," said Tony Quinn, a political consultant and former member of the Fair Political Practices Commission. "Back [in the '70s], the system invited corruption. Orange County cleaned up its act; there are no more crooks. But the structural problems of accountability were never resolved. No one is in charge. It would be like California having a Legislature alone and no governor."

In Orange County, Supervisor Roger Stanton has released his proposal for a county restructuring, in which he called the creation of an appointed county executive officer (CEO) a viable option and made an obscure reference as to whether the treasurer should be an elected position, saying "the rationale of elected department heads must be examined." He also echoed the suggestion of newly elected Supervisor Marian Bergeson, a former state senator, that the county should seek "charter county" status instead of its current general-law status it the flexibility necessary to restructure and to contract with private companies for services that reduce the costs of government.

Quinn says it makes more sense for California to look to a Texas-like system, where a county elects one county judge — who serves much like a mayor — and four supervisors elected by district. He said under this scenario a treasurer would be more accountable, but adds that the treasurer shouldn't be an elected position at all because he or she has little or no accountability.

Barbara Coates, president of the California Association of County Treasurers and Tax Collectors, disagrees, saying because a treasurer is elected countywide, it is that large constituency to whom they are accountable. "Being elected, treasurers have the ability to manage the pool without interference of the board," said Coates, the elected treasurer of Plumas County. "Because of the failure of one county does not mean across the board that treasurers are not doing their jobs or that constituents aren't doing their job to keep qualified people in office. You have to logically evaluate how the county treasurers have been doing their jobs for many, many years."

Coates' group, along with the California State Association of Counties (CSAC), has developed a bill to be introduced in the Legislature that would require candidates for treasurer to meet a minimum level of qualification for the job, institute continuing education standards and establish an oversight committee to review the treasurer's investment activities.

And what is the role of state government in this mess?

Governor Pete Wilson asked a former state treasurer, Tom Hayes, to review the county's portfolio and report on the fund's condition and losses. It was Hayes who determined the fund losses to be $2.02 billion, and a U.S. bankruptcy court ruled that the county could begin selling the securities to prevent further losses should interest rates increase. According to H.D. Palmer with the Department of Finance, the next step is to apportion those losses among the different investors, which include school districts and special districts. He said Wilson has dispatched State Auditor Kurt Sjoberg to handle just that, and he has directed state Treasurer Matt Fong to chair a task force to determine appropriate legislative remedies that could be pursued to assure such financial calamities do not occur again.

But short of providing resources and tools to assess the crisis, Palmer said that the state has no direct responsibility to bail out Orange County. "As far as a blanket policy dealing with counties in financial distress, there isn't one," he said. "In terms of

the investments that were made, there is no excuse for making investments that put county funds at such a high level of risk. It is a wrong presumption for local government entities to go eyes open into highly speculative investments and expect the state to be their deep pockets."

Since passage of Proposition 13 in 1978, California's 58 counties have bemoaned their financial plight and watched their budgets get slashed. They have very little discretion over spending, given that up to 90 percent of county budgets are already spoken for in terms of state and federally mandated programs. Some say the situation in Orange County is a warning shot across the bow for other counties and municipalities that might have begun toying with fast and loose financing strategies to balance the books.

"The Orange County financial earthquake is certainly more than just a warning to other counties to be circumspect about how they do business," said Assemblywoman Marilyn Brewer, a Republican from Orange County and former aide to retired Orange County Supervisor Thomas Riley (see page 18). "The federal government mandates without providing funds, the state government mandates without funds, and this places burdens beyond the capability of counties. We're in an era where government needs to re-examine how it's doing business."

But one source harkens to the 1970s, when local governments had to learn to live with Proposition 13, while Orange County, apparently, refused. "When Prop. 13 hit, the Board [of Supervisors in Orange County] was unwilling to make sacrifices and wanted to maintain a high level of services," said an Orange County politico who asked not to be identified. "Citron was proposing legislation for more flexibility to invest money, the federal government deregulated, he made money and they [board members] looked the other way."

That again raises the question of accountability. In the 1970s, all but one Orange County supervisor, Riley, were indicted after apparently feeling more accountable to campaign-contributing developers than an apathetic voting population. In the years following, there grew a reluctance if not a refusal on the part of elected officeholders to assume oversight of

other elected officeholders. Indeed, evidence that the financial underpinnings of Orange County's investment portfolio were unstable was in the hands of the Board of Supervisors a full year before the last-resort bankruptcy filing last month. But the only input required was that of Citron, and no further questions were asked.

Riley has said the report from a 1991 county audit of the treasurer's office was presented to him as chairman of the board. He recalls having given the report to his key staffer, now freshman Assemblywoman Brewer, for review, and she identified several concerns over some of the auditor's findings. Citron responded in writing to the audit and addressed the concerns brought up by Riley and Brewer. Riley said Brewer read the response and wrote back that everything seemed to be fine. In 1993 the audit and response became public.

For her part, Brewer was unwilling to comment on the report — and her role in approving it. But she was willing to discuss the wisdom of whether or not a treasurer should be elected. She called the notion of an appointed rather than elected treasurer "viable and forward thinking. From my experience within the county structure, if the county treasurer had been appointed rather than elected, there would have been more accountability to the Board of Supervisors. But if they're elected, there is more of a hands-off mentality."

Those in the middle of the fact-finding missions and the immediate survival efforts are too busy to look beyond the tasks at hand. Dennis Carpenter, a former state senator and now a lobbyist representing Orange County, says proposals for a county government restructuring and those that place restrictions on treasurers' investment practices are important but premature. "We are not addressing the issues of the treasurer at this time," Carpenter said. "We're talking about the fiscal impacts and ways to lessen that to meet immediate needs. We've got to clear the decks for life-saving bills."

And indeed, despite quests to lay blame or develop preventive measures into the next century, Orange County and the rest of the state have yet to feel the impact of the county's demise, let alone analyze the extent of the damage. Until then, Californians have another lesson from Orange County. 🏛

ENVIRNOMENT

A once-pristine environmen

Is it too late to save California?

By Tom Knudson

Reprinted from *California Journal*, April 1995

The drive over Brockway Summit on Highway 267 to Lake Tahoe is routine enough. But every time I head over the pass, I hear a distant echo — a voice from long ago: Mark Twain recalling his first glimpse at the bold, blue lake in August 1861.

"As it lay there with the shadows of the mountains brilliantly photographed upon its still surface," Twain wrote in "Roughing It," "I thought it must surely be the fairest picture the whole earth affords."

Today, Twain's words evoke a strange magic: They soothe and they hurt. Celebration has turned to requiem. Lake Tahoe, as everyone knows, is a much different place nowadays. Its dirty air, clogged roads, algae blooms and dying forests have become legendary. But Tahoe's travails are more than a tragedy. They are a parable for our times.

Once, California was the grandest citadel. Its beauty and bounty were beyond belief. Rivers were full of salmon. Skies were draped with waterfowl. Along the North Coast and in the Sierra Nevada, trees grew so huge they seemed extraterrestrial. Majesty was the heart of California. It rumbled through the Big Sur poems of Robinson Jeffers. It was etched onto panels at the State Capitol. It thundered in the prose of California's most famous conservationist, John Muir.

"Climb the mountains and get their good tidings," Muir wrote of his beloved Sierra. "Nature's peace will flow into you as sunshine flows into trees."

But majesty does not build civilizations. People do. Dollars do. Majesty gets lost along the wayside. It doesn't have to but it does. Just look at California.

In the 19th Century, hydraulic miners got their gold but left the foothills scarred and bleeding. Eighty years ago, Los Angeles got water from Owens Valley but turned Owens Lake into a toxic dust bowl. San Francisco dammed the Tuolumne River and Hetch Hetchy canyon. California even killed its state symbol — the grizzly bear. The last one was shot in 1924.

Tom Knudson is Sierra correspondent for The Sacramento Bee. *In 1992, he was awarded a Pulitzer Prize for meritorious public service for his series, "The Sierra in Peril."*

avaged

criminally short-sighted when it comes to resources, ecology and especially sustainability."

But somehow, there is good news, too. While much has been lost, much also remains. One hundred million acres is a lot of ground. California is not yet New Jersey West. On its good days, there is no place finer. The slap of heavy surf on the northwest coast, the distant sparkle of the snowclad Sierra, the rose-tinted dawn over the Mojave desert — all are emblems of a greatness not yet gone.

California is a funny sort of place. It can sadden you one day with its concrete and gridlock. The next day there is a black bear shuffling through your campsite, a bald eagle in your binoculars.

During my eight years here, California has revealed many such surprises. Shorebirds in Death Valley. Salamanders in the Sierra Nevada. A tarantula big enough to stop traffic. A Pacific fisher, one of the rarest, most elusive mammals in North America, 90 miles southeast of Fresno.

Still, as California heads into the 21st Century, there's no denying its problems are enormous. But so is its potential. The challenge is not just to hang on to what remains but to bring back some of the old magic. Get rid of air pollution and California could have the cleanest skies in the nation. The reason? There are no factories or power plants upwind — only the wide blue Pacific and its vast cushion of fresh, clean air.

Rich Pedroncelli

Today, there are new problems — lots of them. Air pollution is causing crop damage in the San Joaquin Valley and fumigating forests in Sequoia National Park. Soil erosion is choking reservoirs and destroying fish habitat. Species are disappearing. California cities have grown so huge that one prominent biologist — Michael Soule at the University of California, Santa Cruz — calls them "centers of extinction."

Southern California is the prototype. Just 60 years ago, the air was scented with orange blossoms and the San Fernando Valley was mostly farmland. No more. Today, the region is growing so fast that, as author Marc Reisner put it, it may run out of air before it runs out of water.

"The fundamental problem," Reisner said in a talk not long ago, "is the human race is devilishly clever but

"If I lived in Ohio, I wouldn't be nearly as enthusiastic," says Tom Cahill, a veteran air-pollution specialist at the University of California, Davis. "Unless we pollute every day, all day, the state would get clean. California is in control of its own destiny."

Our forests could once again be the great cathedrals Muir described a century ago — not the sickly fire-prone thickets they are today. And it need not cost jobs. It could create them. But it will take new thinking, new action. Every year, we spend a king's ransom to put out fire, a pittance to prevent it. Preventative medicine works for our health. Why not for forests?

Preventative medicine means more fire — under controlled conditions — to clear out underbrush and make forests more spacious. It also means biomass harvesting and other kinds of logging and fuels reduction where fire isn't practical.

"It's serious business," says Larry Caplinger, fire management officer on the Stanislaus National Forest. "What we're saying is 'Let's buy some fire insurance for our national forests.' We buy it for our homes. Let's buy it for national forests."

One of the biggest challenges will be safeguarding California's spectacular biotic warehouse. California, even after 150 years of exploitation, is one of the richest biological regions on earth. There are coastal gnatcatchers, delta smelt, fringe-toed lizards, kangaroo rats, yellow-billed cukoos, limestone salamanders, giant garter snakes and several thousand other native plants and animals. No other state has such an inventory.

They are survivors. Native Californians. They have outlasted miners, loggers and dam builders. You might think they would be safe today. You would be wrong. They face new and growing dangers. One of the biggest is close at hand. With 32 million people in the state, native species are simply being shoved aside. Habitat is divided and subdivided until only small islands of open ground remains. Such patches might look pretty but they are prison cells for many species. Cut off from outside populations, they exist in a doomed world — a landscape of the "living dead," says Reed Noss, editor of *Conservation Biology*, a scientific journal.

California's population growth shows no sign of stopping. During most of the 1980s, we grew at the rate of 2000 people a day, a new San Francisco each year. In 1990, a whopping one million newcomers showed up. By 2020, California is expected to have 60 million residents.

"We are losing species and habitats so fast it is almost mind-boggling," says Peter Moyle, a professor at the University of California, Davis, in a remarkable new book about California wildlife, "Life on the Edge" (Biosystems Books). "Southern California seems to have an especially uncontrollable problem. Essentially every species of native fish in Southern California belongs on the endangered species list."

People aren't the only problem. "Alien" species are causing major trauma, too. A Chinese clam brought here inadvertently on a cargo boat is reshaping the ecology of San Francisco Bay. Non-native grasses are pushing out native plants in the Mojave Desert, depriving the desert tortoise of nutrition.

"We are a weed species," the late Wallace Stegner once wrote. "Wherever we go, we crowd out natives and carry with us domesticated species that may become weeds in the new environment. What we destroy we often do not intend to harm. What we import, we import with the best intentions."

Let's say for a moment that you don't care for blunt-nosed leopard lizards or Almeda whipsnakes. You've never seen such things. You may not want to. What good are they anyway?

A fair question. And a tough one. Phil Pister of Bishop has a response. Pister, a retired biologist with the California Department of Fish and Game, has devoted his career to saving little-known creatures, such as the Devil's Hole pupfish. He has heard the "what-good-are-they" question

many times. Each time, he answers the same way: "What good are you?" he says.

There's another response: Because we can.

California, even in a recession, is an economic power-house, a super state. We are part of the world's greatest nation. We send people to outer space, design Star Wars defense systems, watch satellite television. Why not safeguard life on earth?

This shadow world of nematodes and gnatcatchers, diatoms and delta smelt is more important than we realize. They are rivets on an airplane. Lose too many, and you crash. As Paul Ehrlich, professor of biological sciences at Stanford University, says: "When we destroy biodiversity, we're sawing off the limb we sitting on."

Saving biodiversity won't bankrupt us. It will enrich us. You say government doesn't have the money? Well, it seems to have the money for other things. How about those $90,000-a-year do-nothing jobs the State Legislature hands out? Why not cut some of that stuff, and put the money to work restoring watersheds? Why not award tax credits to ranchers who protect streams, who help save condor habitat? Why not put armies of young people, homeless people, welfare recipients to work cleaning beaches, fixing forests, mending ecosystems? What better place to begin than California, with its history as a social innovator, a national trend-setter? The time is right, too, with federal power shifting back to the states.

But alas, these are bleak times for the environment. The talk these days is about gutting conservation laws, not expanding them. Politicians, commodity groups, conservation organizations, all have daggers sharpened and poison in their press releases.

Still, you can find encouraging signs.

Last year, after 15 years of legal wrangling between the Los Angeles Department of Water and Power and environmentalists, Mono Lake was saved by the simplest of solutions: Just add water.

California's Resources Secretary Doug Wheeler is bringing developers and conservationists together to avoid the legal minefield of the federal Endangered Species Act. The centerpiece of the effort, the Natural Communities Conservation Planning Program, is aimed at preserving the once-unknown, now-famous California coastal gnatcatcher.

The Bank of America has joined with the Resources Agency, the Greenbelt Alliance and the Low Income Housing Fund to issue an ambitious state-wide growth-management blueprint for California.

"It is clear sprawl has created enormous costs that California can no longer afford," the groups say in a February report. "Ironically, unchecked sprawl has shifted from an engine of California's growth to a force that now threatens to inhibit growth and degrade the quality of life."

In the north end of the Central Valley, there's more good news: Rice farmers, working with conservationists, have changed farming practices to provide 90,000 acres of winter habitat for waterfowl such as sandhill cranes and snow geese.

Such measures deserve standing ovations. Unfortunately, they don't often get them. Cooperation doesn't grab headlines. But it should. It is getting some attention right here. Right now. Let's see some more of it. 🏛

Photos are from the California Journal *archives and where noted by Rich Pedroncelli.*

Farmers vs. cities

Along State Route 120, the northern highway into Yosemite, there used to be a sign outside the town of Oakdale that read, "Caution: road subject to flooding." I first saw it in August of 1977, the driest month in what tuned out to be the driest year in California history. And the sign wasn't kidding: The highway, though not exactly flooded, was certainly wet.

As one of that day's crop of new California migrants — I had said goodbye to New York's Hudson Valley a couple of weeks earlier — I was thoroughly baffled by the sign, not to mention the water steaming off the skillet-hot asphalt. The landscape I had just driven through was, for my eastern sensibilities, excruciatingly dry; the Sierra forests were wizened by drought, the dun foothills looked scorched. But here in the San Joaquin Valley, whose average rainfall makes Israel seem wet, water flowed everywhere. And it flowed. The highway, I finally realized, had been flooded by the overwash from orchards on either side, where walnut trees stood in shallow lakes.

California's agricultural industry can thank the Oakdale Irrigation District for inspiring me to write "Cadillac Desert" — the book it loves so much. But if their world seems to have begun to implode, the state's farmers — some of them, anyway —

As California heads into the 21st Century, the tug of war over scarce water resources will intensify — a battle that farmers cannot win

By Marc Reisner

Reprinted from *California Journal*, May 1995

might best blame themselves. When Marin County, having curtailed its water use by 60 percent in 1977, was still forced to run an emergency pipeline over the Richmond/San Rafael Bridge, Oakdale's orchard growers kept irrigating by diurnal flood. That Marin had no means of tapping Oakdale's surplus was, from the growers' perspective, the supremely significant fact — not the spectacle of normally wet Marin reverting to desert while large sections of the arid San Joaquin were under water. The farmers' epitaph could thus be written: They Lacked A Sense of Irony.

Recently, the new federal commissioner of reclamation, Dan Beard, tried to explain why his agency's new mandate is largely to referee the transfer of Western water from agricultural to urban use. "When desert cities like Phoenix and Las Vegas and Los Angeles are about to run out of water," Beard said, "they *aren't going to* run out of water. It just won't happen. If agricultural folks say, 'Well, sorry, but we still need all this water to keep raising hay and alfalfa,' well, *that's* just not going to happen. As some sage once said, water does flow uphill toward power and money."

It isn't as if California's $20 billion agricultural industry lacks power and money.

Marc Reisner is the author of "Cadillac Desert," a critically acclaimed book on water in the American West.

Coit Tower mural by Maxine Albro, Journal cover 8/87

It's just that, compared to everyone else, agriculture's had diminished, while relatively speaking its share of the state's water has grown. California has twice as many people as in 1960, when agriculture consumed about 85 percent of the developed water supply; today it still uses 80 percent.

Because big new dams have not been built lately and — except for the odd offstream reservoir — may never be built again, scarcity is finally here. Scarcity creates jealousy, and that 80 percent figure, once a harmless statistic, is now, in the minds of many Californians, a festering injustice. And their grievances go beyond skewed allocation. Why should farmers get taxpayer-subsidized water for $15 per acre-foot when San Diego homeowners may pay a hundred times more for the same amount? One reason is that San Diegans' water is routed through an exquisitely complex and expensive system of aqueducts and pipes, while farm water is simply delivered to canal headgates; but even discounting for that, the disparity in cost is staggering.

Why should commercial salmon fishermen, who represent California's oldest and most threatened industry, face bankruptcy because dams and diversions of water — mainly to agriculture — have reduced a million spring- and winter-run chinook to about 5000 spawners as of last year? Why should urban Californians subsidize the cost of farm water and hydroelectricity, and the cost of flood-control levees, and the cost of flood-related crop damage, and the cost of rural roads they rarely drive, and the disappearance of fish and wildlife, and the social burden of migrant farm workers, and the cleanup of rivers and wells contaminated by selenium and pesticides and salts — and then pay absentee corporations not to raise crops?

On bad days, that is how agriculture looks — some of it, anyway. On good days, the state's farms are a vibrant sector of the economy, a source of gastronomical abundance and variety, and relief from the sanitary horror of urban sprawl. In some places — notably the rice-growing region of the Sacramento Valley — farmland even doubles as good wildlife habitat, especially for waterfowl whose natural habitat has all but disappeared.

Neither perspective is really wrong. And how California's farmers fare in the years ahead will depend, in large measure, on whether their urban brethren are having a good or a bad day.

That urban Californians take a jaundiced view of agriculture is beyond doubt. They didn't always. If anything, Californians used to deify their most prominent rural industry and all the dams and aqueducts that made it thrive. No less a current critic than the *San Francisco Chronicle* was in years past a cheerleader for the Central Valley Project, whose construction led to the subsidies and water diversions and farm-the-government scams it complains about today.

Lately, however, editorial writers at most urban newspapers, not just those in Northern California, have taken swipes at agriculture — especially its unquenchable thirst and seeming indifference, at times, to the ecological harm it has caused. Even *The Modesto Bee*, one of the farm lobby's more loyal friends, was haughtily contemptuous of little Turlock Irrigation District's madcap scheme to build an $800 million dam on the Clavey River, a tributary of the Tuolumne.

By and large, the farm lobby badly misjudged the implications of California's metamorphosis into an overwhelmingly urban state. Statistically, we are now the most urban state in America; in New York, a much greater percentage of the population lives in small towns and villages. In outsize farm towns like Lodi and Tracy, many people — and most of the newcomers — commute to distant

urban jobs. Farmland is something you drive through on your way to work.

Californians' emotional distance from farming has been subversive enough. But environmentalism, the farmers' favorite nemesis, is also an urban phenomenon; it has been since the days when the Republican Party was the party of conservation as well as conservatism and its favorite conservationist, Teddy Roosevelt, was police commissioner of New York City, his place of birth. In New York state, farmers and environmentalists don't often view each other as enemies. But in California, where chronic summer drought makes irrigation necessary, agriculture competes mightily with fisheries, wildlife, wetlands and estuaries — those features of a semi-desert landscape that environmentalists love most.

The day was sure to arrive when all of this regional, cultural, and economic tension between cities and farms would boil out of the pot. That day was probably June 8, 1982, when the Peripheral Canal (Proposition 9) was clobbered at the polls. A much smaller canal would have taken care of urban Southern California's needs, but the San Joaquin Valley wanted an immense one, the better to divert future flows from the rivers of the North Coast. Southern California never spoke of the "need" to dam the North Coast rivers, but the San Joaquin farm lobby did, and that was a huge reason why Northern Californians voted nine-to-one against the plan.

Since that fateful election, the water lobby has continued to pump sand. The valley and the southland, once married through convenience and ambition, have all but divorced. At the same time, the Sacramento Valley, especially its rice industry, has been carrying on an affair with the environmental community, some of whose members — and I am one — are impressed by that industry's conservation record and by the value of ricelands as waterfowl habitat. The San Joaquin Valley, on the other hand, has reacted to this romance as any jilted spouse would. Even in the San Joaquin, "good guy" family farmers raising modestly thirsty, high-value crops such as grapes on small east-side acreage resent lugging the baggage of west-side corporate farms, whose abuses of land, water, and reclamation law have truly poisoned urban attitudes toward farming.

After divorce come settlement and alimony terms, and those were presented in 1992, in the form of the Central Valley Project Improvement Act. Although the mullahs of the agricultural empire portrayed the act as Armageddon, and its co-sponsor, Congressman George Miller (D-Martinez), as the Great Satan, their howls and pleas did not move then-President George Bush, who signed the law prior to a tough re-election fight. The president was more visibly swayed by letters and calls from corporate CEOs, many of them Republicans such as Transamerica's Jim Harvey and Charles Schwab, urging him to sign.

The 1992 act reallocates about a tenth of the project's 8,000,000 acre-foot average yield to wildlife and fisheries; it also tithes CVP customers for a Restoration Fund to recreate habitat. Contract terms are shortened, but subsidies — probably reduced — remain even though farmers had, as of 1987, repaid only $180 million of the billion investment in irrigation facilities alone.

The most interesting language in the improvement act permits transfers of project water anywhere in the state, as long as willing buyers find willing sellers and no more than 20 percent of a district's entitlement is sold. In the past, such transfers were, in effect, illegal. Arguing fiercely against that provision, the farm lobby — with some notable exceptions — abandoned its ideological rugged-individualism and embraced socialism: We want more subsidized water, and we don't want to be allowed to sell it.

The lobby's underlying fear, though not its argument, is worthy of sympathy. Sprawl has inexorably eaten up farmland (see story, page 16) — some of it fabulously good land, like the Silicon Valley — and water transfers to cities can only encourage more sprawl. On the other hand, to paraphrase Commissioner Dan Beard, sprawl will find water one way or another; if it can't buy surplus farm water, it will build dams or tow icebergs.

The water-transfer provision — which was inserted by Beard, who was formerly George Miller's committee chief of staff — actually protects agriculture by capping the amount any district can sell. Since all CVP irrigation water is extravagantly subsidized, much of it is inefficiently used. The fancy prices cities are likely to pay can, in theory, finance conservation improvements that will keep land retirement minimal. Farmers selling land to developers — something the farm lobby rarely opposes — are likely a greater threat to agriculture than water sales.

Like the agricultural industry itself, the improvement act faces an uncertain fate. Some of the extreme provisions in the so-called Contract With America would all but annul its environmental laws, like the Endangered Species and Clean Air acts. A move also is afoot to privatize the Central Valley Project, if anyone can be found to buy what amounts to a gigantic bloc of debt. The betting odds, however, are that the law will survive as well as agriculture. The new general manager of the Metropolitan Water District, John Woodraska, has managed, like earlier perceptive foreigners — he is from Florida — to put California's water dilemma in magnificently simple perspective. "In wet years," he says, "California has

almost too much water. In normal years, there's usually enough for cities and farms, with a decent share for nature. It's mainly in the drought years when there isn't enough.

"If the farmers can get by with 75 percent of the state's water during droughts, instead of 80 percent, then we've basically solved our water crisis."

For another generation, at least, he is probably correct — in theory. The problem is that reality tends to murder theory. 🏛

The runaway train of 1996?

Will an affirmative-action initiative derail Democrats?

By Kirsten Mangold and A.G. Block

Reprinted from *California Journal*, March 1995

I f you took most Democratic candidates off in a corner during the summer of 1994 and asked, "All kidding aside, what do you *really* think of the 'three strikes and you're out' initiative," the chorus chant would have been, "Horrible. Absolutely horrible, and I'm for it four square."

Another profile in courage?

Depends on your definition of "courage," for "three strikes" — on the November 1994 ballot as Proposition 184 — was so popular with likely voters that it became the political equivalent of a runaway train. And no Democrat in a heavily contested election wanted to become a squashed bug on that train's

> **"I don't want to be stuck in '96 with an affirmative-action initiative on the ballot and the Democrats have no alternative to offer but the status quo,"** — Bill Press

headlight. In the end, however, the decision to support Proposition 184 was something of a no-brainer, even for Democrats. After all, who could be against putting scumbags away for life after they'd been convicted of a third felony? Democrats quibbled over the cost for new prisons and over the fact that many non-violent criminals would be snared in the "three strikes" net, but felons — even non-violent ones — were not a base constituency of the Democratic Party and not worth politicide.

But another runaway train may be forming a head of steam for the 1996 election season, and Democrats won't easily finesse their support or opposition to it. This time, the issue is repeal of the state's affirmative-action laws, and it threatens to thunder through the very heart of traditional Democratic constituencies.

Basically, the debate over affirmative-action laws revolves around the question of whether society ought to continue giving preferences to certain groups of people for jobs, educational opportunities and business contracts based on ethnicity, color or gender. Critics say affirmative action has served its purpose and now does more harm than good. Proponents argue that it still is necessary to level the playing field for minorities and women after centuries of discrimination.

For the second time in as many years, affirmative action has been dumped onto the legislative stage by Assemblyman Bernie Richter (R-Chico),

who has sponsored a series of bills and one proposed constitutional amendment, the latter embodied in ACA2. Richter introduced his legislation at the end of January and made it nearly identical to a bill he carried in 1994. That previous attempt failed to get out of committee in the Assembly, but that was an Assembly controlled by Democrats. The new house is split evenly between the two parties.

Richter's package repeals affirmative-action requirements for state agencies, school districts and community colleges, and prohibits public officers from giving preference to applicants based on race, sex, color, ethnicity or national origin. If passed, ACA 2 would go before voters in March 1996 for ratification. As an attempt to amend the constitution, Richter's bill requires a super-majority — 54 votes in the Assembly and 27 in the Senate. As a result, its chances seem slender, even in an Assembly where Republicans have gained parity, because the house still is torn by partisan strife. But there is another element to the effort to repeal affirmative action, one that may have Democrats reaching for the Excedrin: the initiative process. Even as Richter girds for war over his bills, the California Civil Rights Initiative — which mirrors ACA 2 — is being readied for the November 1996 ballot.

For Democrats, it's *deja vu* all over again, a tag team of legislative bill and initiative reminiscent of the effort to pass "three strikes" legislation in 1994. In a legislative debate that could have been scripted by Lewis Carroll, Democrat after Democrat rose on the floor of the Assembly and Senate to say argue that "three strikes" was a rotten piece of legislation. They then proceeded to vote for it.

The affirmative-action initiative, which proponents will try to place on the ballot if Richter's bill fails, also puts an end to all racial and gender preferences in public employment, contracting and college admissions. It's already been endorsed in principle by Governor Pete Wilson and the Republican Party.

The argument to do away with

affirmative action is simple enough: Once there was a time for such a program, and it did what it was supposed to do — give minorities an advantage in a society that long had suppressed them. But now, proponents say, the tables have turned, and perfectly qualified people are passed up for opportunities that go instead to someone less qualified, again because of skin color. "That's as bad as the 'Jim Crow' laws," Richter recently told the *San Francisco Chronicle*. He argues that affirmative-action laws have reached the point of causing reverse discrimination.

This issue seems tailor-made for Republicans, for it appeals to the core of their constituency: the same mostly conservative, mostly white, middle-age male voters who last year backed both "three strikes" and Proposition 187, the successful initiative that curtailed educational, welfare and medical benefits to illegal residents. These also are the same voters who fueled the Republican surge both in California and nationwide.

For Democrats, however, the issue is a minefield — a point acknowledged recently by Assembly Speaker Willie Brown Jr. (D-San Francisco). "It has the potential to be a divisive tool [among Democrats]," said Brown, a self-proclaimed product of affirmative action.

State Democratic Party Chairman Bill Press seemed to echo the potential schizophrenia among Democrats as they approach the issue. On one hand, he expressed raw fear. "I don't want to see a repeat of Proposition 187 ... I don't want to be stuck in '96 with an affirmative-action initiative on the ballot and the Democrats have no alternative to offer but the status quo," he said. "Recognizing that this has the potential to be armageddon in California — far, far worse than 187 — I think we have to look for common ground." Press said that "common ground" could include legislation or an initiative that his party could support, or even a complete overhaul of the affirmative action system.

On the other hand, Press was scornful of Richter's efforts. "Some of the language that I've heard [from Richter] reminds me of David Duke and Ed Meese," he said, referring to the former Ku Klux Klan potentate who ran for governor of Louisiana a few years ago and to President Ronald Reagan's one-time attorney general. "If there's a problem, we're willing to fix it, but the solution is not to go back to the days when white boys ruled."

Repeal of affirmative-action laws poses a quandary for Democrats because it most directly affects some of its most loyal constituencies — women and minorities, especially African-Americans. But the reverberations from an initiative campaign to repeal those laws could echo all down the ticket in November 1996, from President Bill Clinton to those running for the Legislature. Clinton needs California to win re-election, and the last thing he needs is to share the ballot with an initiative that threatens to dominate the campaign and drive a wedge through his own party.

Duane Garrett, state chairman for U.S. Senator Dianne Feinstein's 1994 re-election campaign, said that he is more than a little concerned about this possibility. "If Clinton and the Democratic Party walk the plank of supporting affirmative action, they could lose five or six points in the state," he said. "Clinton can't win without California, and affirmative action is a poison pill for his presidential bid."

In addition, the Democrats' hopes of regaining a majority in the Assembly — and holding one in the Senate — are pegged to winning back several critical Central Valley districts, as well as holding onto marginal seats in the Valley, north coast, San Diego and suburban areas around Los Angeles and San Francisco Bay. These are places where Democrats, for the most part, were clobbered in 1994 and where Propositions 184 and 187 passed overwhelmingly. Like Clinton, Democratic candidates running in marginal areas could be vulnerable should they be forced to take sides on the initiative. If they support it, they risk civil war inside the party. If they oppose it, they face being beaten to a pulp by their GOP opponents.

"There's certainly not going to be a unilateral response within the [Democratic] party," said political consultant David Townsend of Townsend, Hermillo, Raimundo and Usher in Sacramento. "It's like Will Rogers said, 'I don't belong to an organized party; I'm a Democrat.' The party will probably take a position on it, but as was the case with Proposition 187, many Democrats are going to support it or remain neutral. And it's not just the Democrats, either. We've had a political sea change in this country, and we're going to be looking at everything through different eyes."

Townsend is correct when he predicts that both party lines

GOP Assemblyman Bernie Richter argues that affirmative-action laws cause reverse discrimina-

Bernie Richter

Photo by Rich Pedroncelli

may fracture over this, for not all Republicans are lock step behind Richter. For instance, Deborah Wilder, a San Francisco attorney who ran as a Republican in the 12th Congressional District last year, believes Richter's bill is a "broad-brush approach to a situation with individual problems." And she insists that other Republicans agree with her. "... I see this constitutional amendment as abolishing programs that try to create any assistance at all to women or minorities. [Richter] has missed the point that 80 percent of these programs are based on goals, not race."

Wilder says she has written letters to members of the Legislature and has found several Republican allies. She plans to start a coalition against ACA 2, although she is unwilling to divulge names of similar-minded legislators until the logistics have been worked out.

"If you look at the language of this bill, it looks like God, country, mom and apple pie. It's the same bill that was introduced and killed last year, but they took out the harsh language and replaced it with other words," Wilder said, expressing concern that other Republicans — as well as the public — might be so dazzled by the surface appearance of the bill that they might not consider the additional implications.

One other Republican offering a different approach is state Senator Tom Campbell (R-Stanford). "How about taking into account your family's income, or taking into account the first in the family to go to college, or the person who has to work nights?" he told the *Chronicle* in January. "All of that is compassionate, but doesn't use race." Richter has said that he will amend his proposal to allow preferences for college applicants who have been economically disadvantaged. Opponents say that's not nearly enough of an olive branch.

Richter and his allies, however, might not be interested in olive branches. They can review the history of Proposition 184, where proponents used the threat of an initiative as a club hanging over the Legislature. Ironically, proponents put "three strikes" on the ballot anyway, where it passed overwhelmingly.

Wilder knows this same scenario is not out of the question, and she says the possibility concerns her. "It's going to be a hard fight, and an expensive fight. That's why we need to get in on the ground level."

Meanwhile, Democrats must be hoping that this potential runaway train either derails or runs out of steam before it highballs through Democrat Junction. 🏛

The Quest for Community

[Where have you gone, Joe DiMaggio. The nation turns its lonely eyes to you. — Paul Simon]

By Jack Citrin

Reprinted from *California Journal*, February 1995

As the 20th Century lurches to a close, California, once proclaimed as a "Great Exception" immune to the problems of growth, confronts cultural fragmentation, economic uncertainty and political deadlock. No wonder nostalgia reigns, and so many observers contrast a gilded "then" with a tarnished "now." When California truly glittered between 1948 and 1968, they say, people flocked to the state from the rest of the country. Now, some of the same people are leaving. Then, mass migration from the hinterland sustained belief in a common culture based on a comfortable lifestyle; now, immigration heightens ethnic antagonisms. Then, California built schools, universities, highways and water projects; now, it builds prisons and shopping malls. Then, a professional Legislature and competent civil service planned for the future; now, a divided government lacking public trust shrinks from change.

While both the shining "then" and the dark "now" are exaggerated, the slide to the present reality does reflect significant structural changes with enduring implications. The wave of immigration from Latin America and Asia has transformed the state's ethnic profile. Electoral decisions have restricted the power of elected officials to deal with demands emanating from demographic change. The collapse of communism has resulted in a loss of high-paying jobs in defense and related industries, and a concomitant reduction in the government's fiscal resources.

Clearly, national decisions, such as immigration and welfare reform, and international forces, such as the changing value of the peso, will affect the future shape of California's society and constrain its political choices. Nevertheless, the state's own policies in three important domains also will influence how it defines itself as a political community.

On the cultural front, the underlying clash is between the politics of difference and the politics of assimilation. On the budgetary front, the conflict is over how much government should spend, on what and for whom. On the decision-making front, the debate is between restoring the power of representative institutions and further enhancing the processes of direct democracy. Each choice expresses a public philosophy, a distinctive conception of the common good. And each choice tends to favor the interests and values of some ethnic and economic groups at the expense of others. Affirmative-action and bilingual-education programs favor ethnic minorities. Government spending for welfare and public health services help the poor. The majoritarian bias of initiatives and referendums gives an electoral advantage to the preferences of non-Hispanic white voters, who in California are a larger share of the electorate than of the population at large.

Proposition 187 symbolized one combination of choices: more cultural homogeneity, less government spending and more direct democracy. But as the heated debate over illegal immigration showed, the search for common ground in a multi-ethnic society is an exacting task.

Of all issues facing California, coping with ethnic diversity is the most consequential. The 1990 Census reported that the proportion of Hispanic and Asian residents in the state had grown from 25.9 percent to 35.7 percent in a decade, and it is projected that, due to continued immigration and differences in birth rates, by the year 2000, only 50.6 percent of California's population will be non-Hispanic whites. The national trend is similar, though less accentuated. The interplay of this demographic trend with the revival of racial and ethnic consciousness poses a political challenge that may strain the capacities of democratic institutions.

The traditional American solution to the problem of ethnic diversity is what may be termed "liberal nationalism." This doctrine defines American identity in ideological rather than ethnic terms. Whatever one's ancestry or background, to be an American, one has only to adhere to a set of ideals: liberty, individualism and popular sovereignty.

In principle, though often not in practice, liberal nationalism is ethnically inclusive. It asserts that anyone can belong

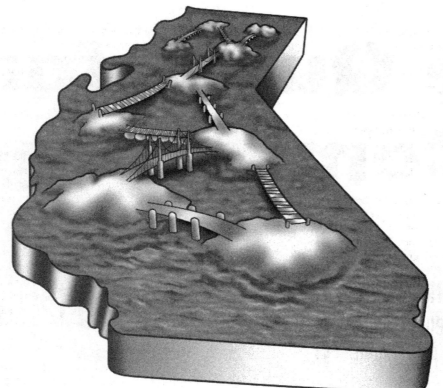

Computer illustration by Perry Babasin

contracts, places in universities, control of the curriculum in schools, legislative seats, time on public television, space in museums, and so forth.

In this context, the census count becomes a paramount political issue. Given the incentive to be designated as part of a group deserving protection from "under-representation," ethnicity can become a strategic option as much as a primordial identity. A recent example is the successful effort of South Asians in San Francisco to gain access to minority set-asides by exiting the Caucasian census category.

A politics of difference must decide how many and which groups deserve recognition and special treatment. The official tendency today is to divide American society into Native-American, European, African-American, Hispanic, and Asian blocs that are assumed to be internally homogeneous. This approach lumps together people, as say Chinese and Filipino residents, with distinctive interests and outlooks, so it may promote demands for a more fine-grained taxonomy of distinct "cultures" and the extension of preferences to these sub-groups. Whatever the system of classification one adopts, whether it creates rather than reflects ethnic divisions, is an important and controversial issue.

The contested meaning of American identity has relevance for current policy choices. For example, because government officials are needed to administer, monitor and enforce the supply of group entitlement, a commitment to affirmative action implies the augmentation of state power. Similarly, a belief in the rights of groups may dictate redirecting public spending to equalize their status.

Immigration is another case in point. Immigration is a highly emotional issue because it defines who belongs to the political community and on what terms. A recent article by Nathan Glazer in *The Public Interest* suggests that one reason for the rise of restrictionist sentiment today is fear that multicultural initiatives in education and language policy will slow assimilation and sow ethnic discord.

Supreme Court decisions in recent years extended many social and political rights to immigrants, thereby reducing the special benefits of citizenship. Non-white immigrants, the current majority, are eligible for affirmative-action benefits denied to either native-born or naturalized whites. Resentment of these developments helped fuel Proposition 187, much as the earlier passage of an "official English" law revealed the staying power of the assimilationist ethos.

The national spread of race-conscious policies resulted from the actions or decisions by judges, bureaucrats and Democratic legislatures insulated from the pressures of mass opinion. The outcome of the 1994 elections, however, indicates that what ordinary people think may matter. This is especially true in California, where the initiative process

and move up the social ladder provided he or she assimilates. The melting pot blends a variety of cultural streams to produce an enriched popular culture without eroding the distinctive ideological core of American identity. Still, immigrants do give up something to achieve acceptance and mobility; their "brutal" bargain means the gradual loss of their original language and customs.

In the vocabulary of contemporary politics, liberal nationalism stands for individual rights, equality of opportunity and the maintenance of minority cultures through the effort of private institutions. It holds that political incorporation for racial minorities and immigrants should occur through citizenship, voting, ticket-balancing and building coalitions within the existing party system.

"Multicultural nationalism" has emerged as a fundamentally different solution to the problem of diversity. The rise of multiculturalism in American politics was sparked by the Civil Rights movement and sustained by the new wave of immigration. In an important sense, it is a response to the persistence of racial inequalities despite legal change.

In contrast to liberal nationalism, multiculturalism construes one's racial or ethnic identity as primary. It upholds the viability and merit of several, equally worthy cultures within the United States. Generally unconcerned about the need for a unifying ideological cement beyond mutual tolerance, advocates of multiculturalism criticize the forces of assimilation that melt down one's ethnic heritage.

By insisting that membership in a particular racial or ethnic group is the ultimate source of one's identity and interests, multiculturalism stands for group rights, equality of outcomes and official recognition for minority languages and cultures. In the political realm, the guiding principle of multiculturalism is communal representation based on numerical strength. In other words, ethnicity should govern the allocation of important benefits such as jobs, government gives citizens the ability to decide specific policies and where ethnic differences in citizenship, registration and turnout boost the strength of white voters.

In activist circles, "identity politics" — the tendency to judge political actions and policies in terms of their impact on the standing of one's own ethnic group — is widespread. The evidence of the polls, however, reveals little support for the multicultural conception of political identity and derivative policies. Ethnic differences in outlook do exist, but these are neither very large nor consistent. Apparently, ordinary citizens continue to believe in the national talent for assimilating diverse peoples.

These conclusions emerge from a Los Angeles County survey conducted in mid-1994. The study is of a restricted sample, of course, but its results are consistent with national and statewide data showing pervasive support for liberal nationalism. A large majority of every ethnic group in the Los Angeles sample said they considered themselves "just an American" rather than a member of a specific ethnic group when deciding political issues. And while a majority agreed that "Americans are greatly divided when it comes to the most important values," this does not imply a belief that ethnicity should define one's identity. When asked whether racial and ethnic groups should "change so they blend into the larger society" or "maintain their own cultures," respondents opted for the melting pot by a margin of 55 to 27 percent.

Linguistic assimilation also was strongly favored. As a group, only Hispanics opposed to a law designating English as the official language of the United States. A majority in all ethnic groups, however, supported policies designed to facilitate the political integration of linguistic minorities: 58 percent of the Los Angeles sample approved of transitional bilingual education programs, and 65 percent agreed that ballots should be printed in languages other than English to help people vote.

Affirmative action has long been a major political battleground. National polls have repeatedly shown support for the abstract principle of racial equality combined with intense opposition to anything that smacks of quotas. The Los Angeles survey similarly found that large majorities of all four ethnic groups disapproved of the idea that "because of past discrimination, minorities should be given preference in hiring and promotion." It did not matter whether the group to benefit was Black, Hispanic or Asian.

Tying political representation to ethnicity also is unpopular, despite the thrust of the Voting Rights Act. A substantial minority of every ethnic group agrees that people are best represented in politics by someone with the same background, but almost no one (13 percent) wants to require that Congress mirror the population at large. Only 8 percent of respondents believed that the racial background of public school and university teachers should closely match the distribution among their students. In allocating desirable social roles, then, ordinary citizens prefer "ability" over "ethnicity."

Despite substantial elitist rhetoric, particularly in universities, and official policies that promote multiculturalism, most ordinary citizens appear unpersuaded. The public remains optimistic about achieving a community in which people share common ideals, speak the same language and advance as a result of individual effort rather than group entitlement. Even among the Hispanic respondents, who display relatively more support for the multicultural policy agenda, there is limited sympathy for maintaining a separate cultural identity on a long-term basis.

Moreover, on both immigration and language issues, including Proposition 187, a variety of polls indicate that the immigrant generation and citizenship status of Asian and Hispanic respondents influence their opinions. As in the past, it seems, integration into American life erodes ethnic differences in political outlooks.

The gulf between elite actions and mass attitudes creates a dynamic situation with a number of potential outcomes. If the politically active stratum were united, one possible trend might be a shift toward more acceptance of institutionalized multiculturalism. The recent Republican ascendancy, however, has strengthened critics of ethnic preferences. An electoral campaign framed in these terms seems bound to increase ethnic polarization at the mass level.

In a society whose population constantly replenishes itself with immigrants from diverse cultures, the inculcation of a unifying identity is a permanent problem. At present, the only solution with broad popular support is a revitalized version of a universalistic and inclusive melting pot. In many respects, America is a more tolerant society than in the past, and agreement on liberal nationalism coexists with respect for cultural pluralism in the private realm.

The alternative conception of the United States as just a container for distinct groups is fueled by the tenacity of ethnically based inequalities. If ethnicity determines the boundaries of a common interest, however, the validation of separateness is unlikely to foster support for equality. Why, one might ask, should I pay for taxes to support someone who claims to be essentially different?

Ethnic cleavages in California overlap with other lines of division: between suburban and urban residents; between economic classes, between "taxpayers" and "tax receivers." In each instance, Blacks tend to be found on the more vulnerable side of the fault line. Race, not immigration or cultural diversity, remains the most intractable political problem.

Over time, citizenship and voting inevitably will speed the empowerment of the rapidly growing Hispanic and Asian communities. There are important differences of values and interests within each of these groups, as well as conflicts between the three main minorities. The pattern of ethnic coalitions thus is likely to vary from issue to issue.

Along with the increasing use of the initiative process in state politics, term limits are likely to weaken the power of incumbent representatives, and the Legislature as an institution *vis-a-vis* the governor. This development may also diminish the power of the residentially concentrated but less-participant minority groups in the near future. In the present institutional context, programs aimed at benefitting minorities will win support only when these policies are framed in ways that affirm rather than attack the dominant conception of American identity.

Harmony in diversity requires some consensus on values. It also requires general confidence in progress toward a better life and in equal treatment. Economic growth remains a solvent for many discontents. To a surprising degree, liberal nationalism remains a powerful ideological glue for most Californians of all ethnicities. The culture wars of the elites are a sideshow in the battles of ordinary life. The task for leadership is to advance the quest for community by moving from symbolism to pragmatism. 🏛

Diversity in higher education

Minority youth have made great strides over the past decade

By Mary Ellen Leary

Reprinted from *California Journal*, February 1995

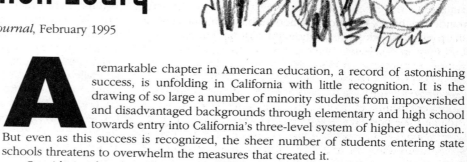

Illustration by Tom Hair

A remarkable chapter in American education, a record of astonishing success, is unfolding in California with little recognition. It is the drawing of so large a number of minority students from impoverished and disadvantaged backgrounds through elementary and high school towards entry into California's three-level system of higher education. But even as this success is recognized, the sheer number of students entering state schools threatens to overwhelm the measures that created it.

Considering the ethnic diversity of the population flooding the state's school system, the high ratio living in poverty — 52 percent of the Hispanic children according to the California Postsecondary Education Commission (CPEC) — and the large numbers

---

Mary Ellen Leary is a veteran political writer who has covered California matters for more than 40 years. She has been a correspondent with The Economist *since 1967.*

involved, the preparation of so many for college-level academia is unparalleled elsewhere. Consider also that a quarter-million of the children in high school are classified as "limited English proficient," needing language training to comprehend their textbooks. One measure of this success is the increase of Hispanics in higher education. In the past decade their numbers among entering freshmen have grown by 70 percent in California community colleges; by 94

The truly astonishing change over the past decade has been the meteoric rise of Asians

percent at the various campuses of the California State University system and by 67 percent at the University of California, as tallied by the commission.

Behind this improvement, spurring it, are a multitude of programs through elementary and high schools: special tutoring, one-on-one encouragement, outreach to parents, peer encouragement. Some are the product of an enterprising individual teacher, some a school district innovation, some the purposeful recruitment developed by a college or university. Even private colleges in the state have built outreach links to local elementary schools and high schools. Stanford's Graduate School of Business, for instance, early on sent volunteer tutors to local grade schools in impoverished neighborhoods.

It may even be counted a measure of success that the high school drop-out rate in California, which used to record about a third of all Hispanic or African-Americans students quitting high school before graduation, now is down to about 20 percent. In terms of sheer numbers, Hispanics who stayed in high school to graduate rose from 38,600 in 1982 to 71,464 in 1993.

Measuring the pursuit of higher education by Hispanic achievement is important because this segment of the population is the fastest-growing and is expected to become a majority of the state's population (see page 22). In pondering the dry statistics of school population, one gets a sharp, even a shocking, realization of the astounding changes occurring in the state's demography — and indirectly its culture. For instance, in 1980 white children numbered over two million, or 53 percent of the state's high school population. Presently they are 42 percent and expected to drop to 30 percent in another decade. Hispanics, on the other hand, will see their portion of the high school population grow from 37 percent to 49 percent over the same decade.

African-Americans and Native-Americans have not been as successful as Hispanics in aspiring to higher education. African-American numbers have declined at community colleges and at UC in the past decade, although they have increased by about 5 percent at CSU campuses. African-Americans last year were about 20 percent of those entering CSU. Today they represent 4 percent of total UC undergradu-

ates. According to the CPEC, one defining drawback African-Americans face is poverty; some 31 percent are from households with incomes below the poverty level. Although Hispanic children also confront poverty, they appear to get more family encouragement in education.

The truly astonishing change over the past decade has been the meteoric rise of Asians. Despite their relatively small proportion of the whole population, they are emerging in dominant numbers in higher education. Last year, for the first time, Asian undergraduate enrollment at UC-Berkeley surpassed that of whites, 35.2 percent to 34.5 percent. At UCLA, Asians have not surpassed whites in total enrollment, but they do outnumber whites among entering freshmen. At UC-Irvine, which specializes in engineering and science, Asians reached 41 percent of undergraduate enrollment, while white students were 35 percent. This is not surprising, since in 1992 over half of all Asian high school students took college preparatory curricula, while just a third of the white students were similarly aiming for college.

For more than 20 years faculty and administrators at all California institutions of higher learning have grappled with ways to instill an aspiration for higher education in minority high schoolers. Back in 1976, UC began "Early Academic Outreach" by which each campus sent staff and volunteers to work with students at schools that had the poorest rates of college admission, guiding them to the proper entry-level courses, tutoring and encouraging them. Last year, this program dealt directly with 56,000 students, according to Dennis Galligani, UC assistant vice president for student academic services. About half were considered ready for higher education when they left high school, many going to CSU and about 25 percent to community colleges.

Another successful effort by UC has been MESA — a program focused on math, engineering, science achievement — which began over 20 years ago at the urging of science faculty and has now spread to community colleges. It also is a mentoring and tutoring effort by university volunteers and staff, last year reaching some 18,000 students. Results have been good; students helped by MESA usually stick with college until graduation.

Some of the most successful outreach efforts have begun through individual teachers. One is AVID — the brain-child of an English teacher in San Diego in the '80s whose high school suddenly saw half its white, affluent, school-attuned pupils replaced by youngsters bused in from the inner city under a court order.

"We had two choices," recalls Mary Catherine Swanson, creator of AVID and now a top administrator in San Diego county's school system. "We could concentrate on remedial work for the minority youngsters. Or we could prepare them to cope with college-directed studies. The latter is what we set out to do."

Assuming that a motivated student could make it, the program's initials stand for "Advancement Via Individual Determination." Essentially, as a student works with tutors and peers in various special classes, he or she gains an enhanced sense of dignity and self-esteem. The program stresses written and spoken expression. Counseling is important, but the key component, which Swanson developed, was recruiting as tutors nearby college students who previously attended the high school. AVID students also work together, egging each other on, learning to ask questions and to prepare for class and tests. In 1992 San Diego found that 93 percent of the AVID students enrolled in college, most of them in a four-year schools. Today the AVID style of teaching is in 125 San Diego county schools, and in another 176 statewide.

Other efforts have cropped up statewide. In San Jose, two teachers at Chabot College were struck by the failure of so many ethnic minority students. Felix Galaviz, a counselor and assistant dean, and Patricia McGrath, an English teacher, hit upon the idea of linking students with individuals in the community from similar ethnic backgrounds to witness successful careers by people with whom they could identify: a Hispanic judge, an African-American librarian, a nurse, a physician, a store manager. Community members were eager to help. The community link was a key, so the program is called "Puente" — a bridge. Puente now is sponsored by UC, and the two innovators have been brought onto the UC president's staff. The program itself has spread across UC campuses and recently into community colleges. A $2 million gift from DeWitt Wallace-*Readers Digest* Fund will enable the UC team to expand to some 18 high schools in the next four years.

Not every innovation is so elaborate. At Claremont Colleges, for instance, one day a year is devoted to inviting fourth-grade children from local elementary schools to visit a campus, walk through admission and classroom experiences, get a cafeteria lunch, and the gift of a T-shirt boasting

"I'm Going to College." In that one day, college students participate in implanting the notion that attending college is attainable.

An independent, privately funded organization in San Jose called the California Higher Education Policy Center seeks ways to respond to the increasing student population, hoping to keep faith in the 1960 dream that any youngster wanting college in California can find a niche. Disturbed by the effect of recent cuts in state funding for higher education, along with increases in student fees, it urges changes in university time schedules to reduce cost; for instance, teaching classes year-round, and on weekends and nights might fulfill the need for space without undertaking new construction. Another education reform center is under preparation at CSU-Sacramento, where former state Senator Gary Hart (D-Santa Barbara), long an expert on education, will preside over an institution looking especially at teacher training.

There are obstacles in the way of continued encouragement for minority access to higher education, however. The state's fiscal problems have meant recent cuts in budgets plus increases in student fees. These have been blamed for a decided enrollment drop last year, especially in community colleges and at CSU. The governor's 1995-96 budget promises a small improvement, as does the economic good news.

But another hazard is powerful public antagonism towards immigration, an outgrowth of the Proposition 187 campaign to bar illegal immigrants from schooling. Although the majority of Hispanic high school students are second- or third-generation Californians, the political alarms about illegal entries spill over into all ethnic concerns, and worry those in education.

There also have been some recent criticisms of minority student performance in college. CSU administrators have protested the amount of remedial work colleges must undertake with poorly prepared students who are admitted but are not up to expectations. This could build into a serious crisis over low-achieving pupils who seek higher education. In addition, a UCLA professor of education, Alexander Astin, said a nationwide study suggests a problem with "grade-inflation" at the high-school level.

Galligani says Astin's worry doesn't apply to California, while at UC-Berkeley, Greg Thomson, director of student research, said the success in educating students from lower socio-economic backgrounds can be proven "in objective test scores, in strictly professional evaluations. ...Compared to classes a decade ago, UC-Berkeley freshmen are substantially stronger from top to bottom."

But the tide of increasingly larger classes is swamping many remedial efforts. Said Barbara Brandes, who heads the state Department of Education's high school division: "We are at a point where individual student help is no longer a workable solution. Some systemic reform must be made in our school system. The big question is whether we must abandon the initial idea that formed our system in the '60s and had contributed so much to the state's economic advancement — the concept that every California child should have the chance to attend higher education, at one of the three levels the state provides. Or do we direct high school learning more towards job-training, which is likely to leave youngsters from low-income families headed for low-pay jobs. This is the issue on which debate is sharpest in educational circles today. It is a very disturbing time." 🏛

Revised California's Budget Dance

Issues and Process
2nd Edition
By Richard Krolak

California's $57 billion budget is where the action is when it comes to programs and policy in the nation's largest state. Education, taxation, environmental protection, transportation, social services, local government support — you name it and the budget addresses it.

But the process is complicated, often seeming murky to the uninitiated.

The solution is *California's Budget Dance*, a 150-page book that describes the state's economic environment and the budget process.

All this for only $9.95. To place your order call or write *California Journal*, 2101 K Street, Sacramento, CA 95816. Phone (916) 444-2840.

Education

Crime issue knocks education out of the spotlight

Laura A. Locke

Reprinted from *California Journal,*
February 1994

Last November, many connected with public education in California were genuinely excited about the promise of 1994. The special election on the fate of Proposition 174, the school voucher initiative, had brought the state of K-12 education into a sharper political focus than it had enjoyed for several years. Despite the ringing defeat of their costly and controversial measure at the polls, voucher proponents reminded voters that there was work to be done in the state's schools. Opponents, victorious though they were, were forced to concede that the public's judgment was not a ringing endorsement of the status quo.

Within weeks of the voucher vote, everyone who was anyone in California's political elite weighed in on the subject. Governor Pete Wilson offered up a multi-point plan for school improvement on the very day of the election. His plan included retaining a hired-gun consultant (or, in Wilson's words, "education ambassador") named Dr. Frank Newman, who runs a Denver-based education think tank. State Treasurer Kathleen Brown, considered the favorite for the Democratic nomination for governor, also came up with a multi-point plan for school reform.

What a difference a few months can make. As the solid defeat of school vouchers fades into the background, it appears education already is being eclipsed by crime and the state budget as issues of primary public and political concern. A measure of how far schools have slipped off the radar screen came in the governor's recent State of the State address: Education merited not one word of mention in a 35-minute speech. Administration officials said there just "wasn't time" during the speech, though the governor did find time to plug his "crime summit," then slated for mid-January but canceled after the Los Angeles earthquake.

"The educational system of this state is over half of the state's budget," said Democratic Assemblywoman Delaine Eastin of Fremont. "I do not know how you can talk about the state of the state and fail to discuss what's going to happen in education. It's an outstanding omission."

• If school reform is to again fall through the political cracks, it won't be because it wasn't urgent enough. According to a survey commissioned by Policy Analysis for California Education (PACE), an independent education policy research group, nearly nine out of 10 Californians believe schools need to be changed, and more than two-thirds believe a complete overhaul is in order. The lopsided numbers are not surprising, considering the challenges facing this $30 billion behemoth.

• Of the five million-plus kids who attend school in California, more than a million are limited English-proficient;

• California ranks next-to-last among the 50 states in class size, and has spent time at the bottom of the heap;

• According to the National Assessment of Educational Progress, California students rank near the bottom in reading achievement;

• California schools spend nearly $800 less per-student than the national average, despite having to support the seventh-highest teacher salaries in the country;

• For the first time since the early 1980s, the proportion of high-school students taking the college-prep requirements for the University of California declined.

What makes school reform so elusive is that nobody can quite agree on the target. Terms like "education reform" and "restructuring" are continuously bandied about, but the terms mean different things to different people. Some reformers, like those who backed last year's voucher initiative, center their attention on the governance of schools and school districts. Reformers within the system — such as teachers' unions, administrators and school boards — tend to focus their gaze on finances (or lack thereof). Still others, particularly in the religious community, target curriculum reform as their top priority. "Reform" also covers such topics as revamped textbooks, educational technology and even self-esteem courses.

Semantic distinctions are not the only roadblocks to reform. Education has been polarized and paralyzed by a complex web of political agendas — sometimes interlocking, sometimes conflicting. In high-profile fights, such as those involving funding or last year's voucher campaign, key interest groups such as teachers and administrators band together, forming what's euphemistically described as "the Unusual Coalition." When it comes to the details of reform, however, these interests splinter and spin to reflect their own self interest. Talk to the California Teachers' Association, the state's largest teachers union, and you'll hear a lot of talk about the "respect" their profession deserves. Talk to the California School Boards Association, and you're likely to hear more about fiscal and professional "accountability."

Then there is the practical side of reform; in other words, how do you pay for it? The last three years have seen schools fighting just to keep the money guaranteed them by 1988's Proposition 98 school-funding initiative. For the past two years, Governor Wilson has kept education spending just above the Proposition 98 minimum funding level, in part by a series of "loans" against future funding. The CTA has challenged the scheme in court. Although there were no additional cuts in the 1994-95 spending plan, no adjustments were made for inflation or increasing enrollment demand on a system burdened with 150,000 new students who enter state schools annually. The CTA says that's a cut any way you slice it.

It all seems so insurmountable that it isn't hard to see why reform has moved so slowly. In fact, with so many political crosswinds buffeting its docks, what's really remarkable is that schools can make any progress toward improving their quality. Yet, progress has been identified, primarily as a result of the last significant wave of reform. In 1983 the Legislature passed Assembly Bill 813. The 214-page law offered 83 separate improvements, including tougher curriculum, broader testing, and a renewed emphasis on the basics. The groundbreaking reform effort, was prodded by the release, in April of 1983, of "A Nation At Risk", the political firebomb lobbed by President Ronald Reagan's National Commission on Excellence in Education. The report has been defined by its cataclysmic rhetoric about "a rising tide of mediocrity" in the nation's schools that, if imposed by a foreign country, would be considered "an act of war."

Although progress has been hampered by the tightening budget screws, measurable improvement has occurred in several areas. The school year was lengthened to 180 days.

Textbook protocols were updated, forcing publishers to upgrade the content of textbooks or risk losing out on a share of the lucrative California market. Statewide graduation requirements were implemented along with more vigorous model curriculum standards. Among the most significant achievements is the fact that the statewide dropout rate declined more than 30 percent between 1986 and 1992. Math and science test scores also have stabilized, particularly among middle school and junior high school students.

While they concede strides have been made, many education leaders insist schools are a long way from hitting the tape in the race for reform. "Not as much is happening as I would like to occur," says Gary Hart, chair of the Senate Education Committee.

What would Hart like to see happen?

For starters, more charter schools and broader public school choice. Hart has carried legislation in both areas, which share the common theme of introducing a competitive element into education. Charter schools are designed as individual self-contained entities, stripped of many of the more onerous bureaucratic constraints. The goal is to give professionals a chance to test different approaches — one might be strictly college prep, while another might be an arts and performance school. Public school choice goes even further, offering students and parents a chance to cross district boundaries in order to send their children to any school they wish, space permitting.

In the past, Hart's efforts have butted up against the education establishment, especially the CTA. The union, however, softened its opposition to charter schools and has even been less openly hostile to public school choice. Why? According to CTA president Del Weber, policymakers have sought CTA input as the reforms are being developed. "None of the [past] reform efforts have ever taken teachers out of the classroom and asked for teacher input," says Weber. "CTA has only been asked to react and respond."

On a more practical level, however, CTA's new tone may have less to do with a change of heart than a change of circumstances. In surveying its membership, CTA has found that the concerns of teachers extend far beyond salaries, fringe benefits, and protection of collective bargaining — the traditional union bailiwicks. Teachers are also desperately concerned about the conditions in which they operate. When it makes its case to the education summit, CTA will emphasize these aspects of reform, as well as those involving curriculum and funding. "It's in our best interest to have this work," says Weber, "otherwise we're going to have another voucher initiative on the ballot."

Ah, yes: vouchers.

The specter continues to haunt the education community despite having polled barely 30 percent support in last November's special election. True believers in Proposition 174 have remained remarkably undaunted by the magnitude of their defeat and are already loading up for another try.

Meanwhile, as the physicians argue over the right prescription, the patient's condition grows worse. Some suggest that, if the slide continues, education's role as a unifying democratic institution could collapse.

"Education is only one of several ways the state influences where we are going to be in the 21st century," says San Jose-based education consultant Patrick Callan. "If we fail to effectively make this collective investment in our kids, then California may no longer be conducive to being a prosperous and humane place." 🏛

PAY AS YOU GO

Privatizing California's "Public" Higher Education System

By Steve Scott

Reprinted from *California Journal*, March 1994

illustration by Christopher

Posterity will record that history was made twice during the third week in January 1994. At the beginning of the week, the state's most expensive natural disaster struck the San Fernando Valley in the form of a magnitude 6.8 earthquake and a seemingly unending string of aftershocks. At the end of the week, a different kind of aftershock tumbled out of a San Francisco meeting of the University of California Board of Regents. With only two dissenting votes, the 25-member board took an unprecedented step. They didn't admit that they'd taken it. The university's administration, in fact, explicitly denies that they've taken it. Nonetheless, by all but the most ephemeral semantic criteria, the University of California adopted a policy toward resident students that its founders would have considered unthinkable.

It began charging them tuition.

The barrier was crossed not when the board approved a $620 increase in "student fees" for the coming fiscal year. It wasn't crossed when they also approved a multi-year fee plan that could, by 1996, push UC student fees from the current $3700 a year to more than $5400 a year. No, the psychological line in the sand was erased with the adoption of an accompanying policy change which, for the first time, explicitly permits the use of student fee money to help pay "instructional expenses," including faculty salaries. The new policy effectively breaks the "no tuition" compact at the cornerstone of the 1960 Master Plan for Higher Education, which proposes fees only for non-instructional, "support" services.

For many involved with higher education, however, the change at UC is the clearest symbol yet of how far California has strayed from the public higher-education utopia of the Master Plan — accessible, affordable higher education for every adult who can benefit. Consider the following:

• Governor Pete Wilson's new state budget proposes a $7 per unit community college fee increase. If approved, full-time community college students will pay $600 a year, or about as much as it cost to go to a California State University campus just six years ago.

• Last year, the CSU Board of Trustees approved a four-year fee-increase structure designed to increase student fees to one-third the cost of instruction. If fully implemented, that means fees could rise as high as $2400 a year by 1997, or a four-fold increase in just nine years.

• Enrollment in public higher education in the state last year dropped by 160,000, or 8 percent, far and away the largest drop in the nation. Most of that enrollment decline was in community colleges, which lost 137,000 students.

• If the UC price structure approved by the regents is fully implemented, "fees" at the university in 1996 will be roughly three times what they were when Wilson took office in 1990.

The guardians of UC, CSU and the community colleges maintain the dramatic fee hikes are simply a reaction to the collapse of the California economy and to the shrinkage in state revenue available for higher education.

Officials also maintain that, even with the fee increases, students in California still get a better deal than their counterparts in other states. According to the state Department of Finance, fees at both CSU and UC remain lower than those for resident students at competing institutions in other states. Wilson himself says the two systems remain "a good deal" despite the escalation in fees. The administration makes an even stronger case for the community colleges, which have historically had the nation's lowest fees. If Wilson's proposed $7 per unit fee hike is approved by the Legislature, community college fees will still, according to the administration, be the third lowest in the nation.

Comparisons with other states, however, are little comfort to the students and parents who are writing larger checks or borrowing more. According to the California Student Aid Commission, California college students took out a record $1.24 billion in new loans in the last six months of 1993 — a 50 percent jump over the same period in 1993. Other students find themselves working longer and longer hours, and some risk being priced out of college altogether.

As the check gets larger, meanwhile, course and section offerings diminish. Thousands of course sections have been cut system-wide at CSU, forcing an increasing number of students to extend their education an extra year in order to meet their major's course requirements.

Since 1990 community colleges have reduced the number of course sections by 10 percent. More specialized courses — such as certain foreign languages, design and graphic arts — were eliminated to make way for more offerings in core courses, such as math, science, and English.

It doesn't take an economics major to figure out what happens when fees go up and course offerings go down: students bail. Enrollment at CSU dropped 6 percent last year, with 22,000 fewer students attending classes — 13,000 of them full-time students. UC lost only 2 percent of its 125,000 students in 1993, a change not surprising given that UC students tend to come from more affluent homes than those attending CSU. Most shocking was the decline in enrollment at community colleges — down 137,000 students, or 9 percent of the more than 1.5 million attending these schools.

What makes the enrollment drops at CSU and community colleges especially striking is that they occur at a time when the pressure for increased enrollment should be overwhelming. Not only is the state's population growing, but fee increases at the more expensive institutions have traditionally fueled enrollment at the less expensive schools. The economic downturn itself should have caused community college enrollments to soar, as those forced out of work by the recession go back to school for retraining. Yet, the trend continues downward.

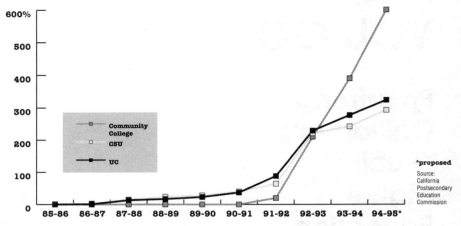

A Decade of Growth in Undergraduate Student Fees

*proposed

Source: California Postsecondary Education Commission

Recognizing the barriers to access that can be created by sharp fee increases during a recession, all three systems have accompanied their hikes with hefty increases in financial aid. Since 1990 roughly one-third of every additional fee dollar has gone into the financial aid pool at UC, CSU and the community colleges. UC Regent William Bagley says the fee increases have allowed the university "to provide full aid to cover the needy student." Financial-aid dollars have doubled at community colleges since 1990, and CSU officials claim a more than five-fold increase over the same period.

Critics say the financial aid backfill doesn't nearly make up for the impact of the fee hikes, particularly on middle-income students. While UC enrollment of low-income students has risen from 25 percent to 29 percent, the university has lost students with family incomes in the $50,000 to $70,000 range. Changes in the eligibility criteria, including a recent one more closely tying aid to parents' income, have hit students especially hard.

Student groups also believe the colleges and universities haven't done enough to cut administrative and non-essential costs. The issue is particularly touchy at UC, where critics have long charged that professors don't spend enough time in the classroom. "There are cost-containment efforts on campuses, but there's no system-wide commitment to cost containment," says Sara Swan with the UC Students Association. "They're only looking at fees."

Officials in all three systems vigorously deny that they've ignored cost containment. UC claims to have cut nearly half a billion dollars from its budgets over the last four years, and UC President Jack Pelatson says the institution is undergoing "a serious restructuring of the way we go about our business." CSU's downsizing in course offerings has been accompanied by a significant administrative downsizing.

Still, the criticism resonates in the ears of the CSU Board of Trustees and the UC Regents, who make the policy decisions and must face the phone calls from frustrated students, parents and legislators. Before voting for the new UC fee policy, several regents made it clear they are watching the administration closely, and expect fee rollbacks to be the top priority if more state dollars become available.

Much of this rhetorical thrust-and-parry, of course, is for the benefit of the Legislature and the governor, who have the ultimate power to shape student fee policy. Last year, CSU's four-year master fee plan suffered a setback when the Legislature chopped its 37 percent fee increase to 10 percent.

What's left for policymakers, then, is the same awful conundrum — hike fees and further threaten access, or roll fees back and possibly threaten the value of the degree itself. With those in charge of higher education continuing to insist that there's no fat left to be cut, students and their advocates see nothing but more and larger fee increases in the years ahead. These increases, they believe, will further strain the already tenuous link between the vision of the Master Plan and the realities of the recession-ravaged 1990s. 🏛